HIKING TRAILS III

Central and Northern Vancouver Island and Quadra Island

Featuring hiking routes

of Strathcona Park

and

for the first time

Quadra Island

and the

Campbell River area

OLYMPIA BRANCH
THE MOUNTAINEERS

EIGHTH EDITION, 1996

Published by

Vancouver Island

Trails Information Society

Revised and edited by

James Rutter

COMOX GLACIER

Eighth Edition Copyright © 1996
Vancouver Island Trails Information Society
(name change only)

Originally compiled and
edited by Jane Waddell

ISBN 0-9697667-1-8

Revised and reprinted 1975
Revised and reprinted 1977
Revised and reprinted 1979
Revised and reprinted 1982
Revised and reprinted 1986
Reprinted with revision notes 1990
Revised and expanded 1992
Reprinted 1994
Revised and expanded 1996

SEPTIMUS

WATERFALL
ON SCHOEN

ELKHORN

COLONEL FOSTER

Word Processing by James Rutter Consulting
Map revisions by A.N. Fraser Drafting Services
Printed by Hemlock Printers Ltd., Burnaby, BC
Distributed by Orca Book Publishers
PO Box 5626, Station B, Victoria, BC, V8R 6S4, Canada

CAPE SCOTT

ACKNOWLEDGEMENTS

Base maps, printed in grey and blue, have been reproduced using overlays from National Topographic Series colour maps ©Her Majesty the Queen in Right of Canada, with permission of Energy Mines and Resources Canada.

Other maps, and information printed in black, have been prepared for this book by Arnold Fraser of A.N. Fraser Drafting Services.

Thanks to the principal contributors to the original version of this book: John S.T. Gibson, John W.E. Harris, Dan Hicks, Ruth Masters, Jack Shark and Syd Watts, and to the many others who contributed to the original compilation and to subsequent revisions.

Special thanks to the following who have contributed to this revision: Sandy Briggs, Lindsay Elms, Ross and Deborah Camp, Noel Lax, Ruth Masters, Murray McLeod and Steve Smith.

The following have helped us in many different ways and we are most grateful: BC Forest Service, BC Parks, Canadian Forest Products Ltd., TimberWest Forest Ltd., MacMillan Bloedel Ltd., Nimpkish Valley Search & Rescue Team, Outdoor Recreation Council of BC and Western Forest Products Ltd.

With special thanks to the Editorial Committee and the other Society members: Joyce Folbigg, John W.E. Harris, George Kelly, Susan Lawrence, Jane Toms, Ron Weir, Betty Burroughs and Aldyth Hunter.

Illustrations by John S.T. Gibson.

Cover photograph: Hikers in the upper Elk River valley, with the south side of Elkhorn Mountain in the background.

Uncredited photos throughout the book: courtesy of James Rutter.

LIST OF MAPS

CONTENTS

SECTION 3: AREAS OTHER THAN STRATHCONA PARK

Phillips Ridge in late July,
looking northwards to Golden Hinde and The Behinde.

LEGEND

Contours are either at 40-metre or 100-foot intervals.

Throughout these maps we have used the following legend:

———————	Public road or highway
——— — ———	Gravel or dirt road
— — — — — —	Clearly defined trail
••••••••••••••••	Hiking route requiring map and compass (experienced hikers only)
⚐	Provincial Park campground
▲	Campsite with pit toilet
△	Backcountry campsite (no facilities)
⊙	Memorial cairn
▪	Cabin
Ⓣ	Toilet only
Ⓦ	Water source
⚒	Mine
P	Parking

Circled numbers on maps refer to notations in the text.

1

GENERAL MAP

CENTRAL AND NORTHERN
VANCOUVER ISLAND

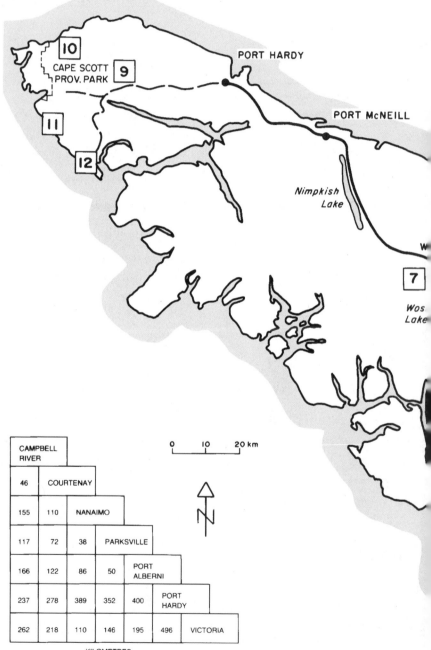

PORT HARDY

CAPE SCOTT
PROV. PARK

PORT McNEILL

Nimpkish
Lake

Wos
Lake

CAMPBELL RIVER						
46	COURTENAY					
155	110	NANAIMO				
117	72	38	PARKSVILLE			
166	122	86	50	PORT ALBERNI		
237	278	389	352	400	PORT HARDY	
262	218	110	146	195	496	VICTORIA

KILOMETRES

0   10   20 km

N

KEY TO MAPS OF TRAILS AND ROUTES

A0-E5	Strathcona Provincial Park
1(a-f)	Campbell River Area
2(a), 2(b)	Quadra Island
3	Snowden Demonstration Forest
4	Seal Bay Regional Nature Park
5	Sayward Forest
6	Upana Caves
7	Nimpkish Valley Area
8	Schoen Lake Provincial Park
9(a)	Marble River
9(b)	Port Hardy/Holberg Area
10(a), 10(b)	Cape Scott Provincial Park
11	Raft Cove Provincial Park
12	Grant Bay

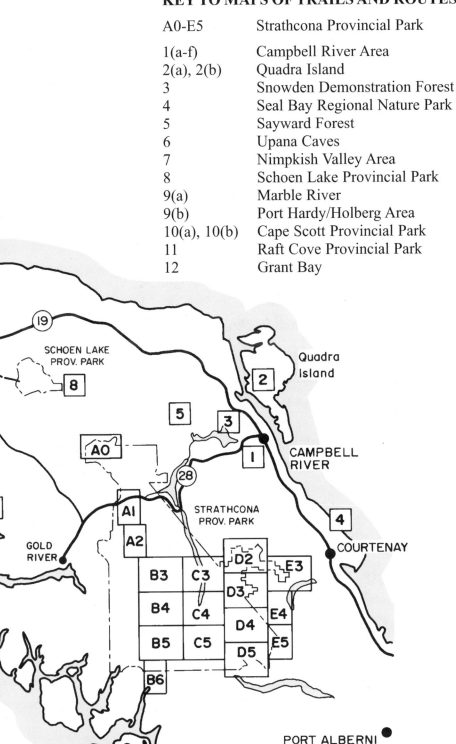

EDITOR'S NOTE

Surely the 90s will be known as the time when the importance of conservation, whether of the environment, biodiversity or natural resources, became an international priority. You, the readers of this book, are probably used to separating your household garbage into compost, recyclable materials or true rubbish. Products which are environmentally-friendly are often preferred, and most cars are now designed to require lead-free gasoline. A new social awareness, of how humankind impacts our Earth and its interdependent natural systems, continues to change our attitudes, habits and lifestyles. Are you equally aware, as you hike through Vancouver Island's most beautiful wilderness areas, of the impact you have on these fragile and sensitive ecosystems?

Twenty years ago, in the first edition of this guidebook, the original authors stated "It is with some misgivings that we publish these details as the high alpine areas can be damaged by over-use and above all by thoughtless camping practices." Their concern was well founded. Today, Strathcona Park is experiencing more use than ever before, and some areas are literally being loved to death.

Fortunately, most visitors limit themselves to frontcountry areas, where BC Parks' staff have a mandate to mitigate user impacts by, for example, building trails, designating camping areas, providing toilets and restricting the use of campfires.

The Master Plan for this park, developed with a great deal of public input, designates most of the backcountry area to "wilderness conservation". While this ensures against float planes and helicopters landing there, it is a category which doesn't permit BC Parks to do any maintenance, provide any facilities (including toilets) or even place signs. In fact, these backcountry areas are solely dependent on their isolation for their continued preservation.

This means that if **you** travel a backcountry route in Strathcona Park, **you alone** bear the responsibility for how much you impact the area. Obviously, this can only work if all hikers passing through ensure they leave no lasting trace.

Fortunately, the current climate is towards no-trace camping rather than the bough beds and campfires of the pioneers.

Because each footstep and tent site adds to your impact, backcountry groups should be small in number. At heavily-used locations, such as Forbidden Plateau and Bedwell Lake, you are encouraged to make a day visit rather than an unnecessary overnight camp.

A concern to preserve Strathcona Park's wilderness experience has led the hiking community to adopt the convention of not building cairns or flagging routes. Not only are such signs unwelcome evidence of human activity in otherwise pristine places, but leaving such markers may lead others into areas beyond their competence.

This edition includes a number of areas we have not described before, in particular the trails and routes of Quadra Island and the Campbell River area. The hikers who live on Quadra have been very generous with sharing their special places and the trails they have developed. You will find yourself welcomed there, but please, ensure your continued welcome by exercising your low-impact hiking and camping techniques wherever you go.

This guide will help you to discover the joys of hiking, but it is a hikers' guide only and it will not show you how to climb the highest peaks. That you have to do for yourself. Instead we emphasize a need for self-reliance. Self-reliant hikers will have an experienced leader, and also the right maps, a good compass and the know-how to use them both. They will also carry a first aid kit, some overnight survival gear and be able to deal with any emergency.

This guide book is written in that same spirit, and provides a key to the door - beyond which you are on your own. It is very important that you read the text rather than simply try to follow the dots on our maps. Though brief, the route descriptions are perhaps the most valuable part of this book. Every word was written by someone who was there, and who experienced the same difficulties facing you. As you enjoy these trails and routes, may you hike safely **and** step lightly.

James Rutter, January, 1996

HOW TO USE THIS BOOK

This book describes trails and wilderness routes including, for the first time, a lake system canoeing route, in some of the most beautiful areas of north and central Vancouver Island.

We make no attempt here to recommend the sort of equipment, clothing or food that a backpacking trip entails, as there are many books and catalogues available which do this, and other enthusiasts to offer you conflicting opinions. Preparing for a trip can be as much fun as the trip itself and we hope we are supplying here something to help you properly do your homework on route and trail conditions **before** setting out.

Our text should be read in conjunction with our maps, and also the corresponding National Topographic (NTS) 1:50,000 maps. References to altitude and compass directions are frequently used to pinpoint position. Wherever the text references a specific location with a raised number like this: Tatsno Lakes [47], a corresponding circled number will be found on a map in this book. Metric conversion is approximate. Times given are average group times as taken over the years by experienced parties, carrying packs.

We will not be held responsible for any discrepancies, inaccuracies or omissions as conditions and road access are constantly changing. Hikers always travel at their own risk and it is up to the individual to check current conditions.

For the benefit of newcomers to hiking, a trail is a way which may have been built by man or travelled regularly by animals so it is obvious. Trails are sometimes signed, marked with cairns or flagged with tape. Routes indicate a possible way to go, though on the ground there may be nothing to see, except the lie of the land as understood by an experienced hiker. Our maps show trails and routes, and only experienced hikers or groups with very experienced leaders should attempt to follow the routes.

Vancouver Island Trails Information Society

HINTS AND CAUTIONS

Recreational use of forest lands is now an accepted part of forest management. While most of British Columbia's provincial forest land is owned by the public, it is leased and managed by forest companies. Recreation (camping and picnicking) sites and trails are developed by the BC Forest Service, and forest industry companies, on provincial forest lands managed for multiple use. Within provincial parks, BC Parks is developing campsites in order to focus the impact of an ever-increasing number of visitors, many from other countries around the world.

Visitors, and those venturing into northern Vancouver Island's backcountry areas for the first time, may appreciate the following selection of hints and cautions. In fact, we suggest that even experienced hikers will benefit from some of our quick reminders.

Access information on logging roads may be obtained from company division offices, tourism offices or from BC Forest Service offices (see page 11). Ask for a "Recreation and logging road guide to the forest lands of Vancouver Island". Due to problems with narrow roads, vandalism or fire hazard, access to logging roads is often limited. Roads may be "**open**", with travel permitted at all times; "**restricted**" (limited), with travel permitted only during non-working hours (normally from about 5:00 pm to 6:30 am, and on week-ends and holidays); or "**closed**". The limitations on access to any particular road may change frequently with little notice. Holidays are sometimes worked. Roads are generally closed when fire hazard is high, or are open only in the mornings, even when general BC Forest Service closures are not in effect. A long distance call a day or two in advance of a trip is often a worthwhile investment. Obey signs: open gates may be locked later when you need to leave.

An understanding of **logging road systems** may help travellers find their way. Typically, various branch and spur roads from higher elevations join to form main roads which lead down to tidewater or mill. Roads may or may not be well marked. Main roads and branches are usually given sequential numbers and/or letters, i.e. Mainline East 200 (in this case there will probably also be a

West 200) might have BR 210, 220 and 230 joining it, in that order, and the latter might have BR 231 off it, with BR 231A off BR 231.

Always have headlights on when **driving dirt or gravel roads**. The safest procedure to follow, when a logging truck is approaching, is to pull well over to the side of the road and wait until it passes. Always yield to loaded trucks, particularly on narrow roads and when they are travelling downhill. This may mean backing rapidly to a turn-off. Trucks often travel in groups...so don't be in a hurry to pull back onto the road after one has passed.

Exercise special care in remote areas. Many areas in this book are out of reach of immediate help in emergencies. Most logging vehicles carry radios and there are telephones at logging camps, but the major parks do not have offices and the trails are generally not patrolled regularly by park staff. Gasoline is not available away from main public roads and towns.

Current information on provincial parks is available from: BC Parks, 800 Johnson Street, Victoria, BC, V8X 1X4 (phone: 387-6804). Maps are also available from offices of some of the major logging companies and/or from tourist information offices.

Maps: A topographic (contour) map and aerial photograph are useful adjuncts to the trail descriptions in this booklet. For the hiking route section they are essential. Maps showing contours are most useful for determining where you are, as you can readily assess steepness, spot creeks and ridges, and calculate the effort that will be required. A contour line is simply all the points of the same elevation joined together; so when contours are close together the terrain is steeper than where they are farther apart.

National Topographic Series (NTS) maps at a scale of 1:50,000 (2 cm = 1 km) are probably the most useful for hiking on Vancouver Island. NTS maps have been used for the base maps in this book. You should purchase your own because we have not reproduced all their information - e.g. NTS maps show forests in green, and treeline is a good navigational map feature.

NTS maps are available from:

Geological Survey, Canada, 100 W. Pender, Vancouver   666-0271
Worldwide Books & Maps, 736A Granville Street, Vancouver   687-3320
Crown Publications, 521 Fort Street, Victoria   386-4636
Robinson's Sporting Goods, 1307 Broad Street, Victoria   385-3429
Island Blue Print Co. Ltd., 905 Fort Street, Victoria   385-9786
*Nanaimo Maps and Charts, 8 Church Street, Nanaimo   1-800-665-2513
Mountain Meadows Sporting Goods, 368 Fifth St. Courtenay   338-8732
Spinners Stores, 1131 Tyee Plaza, Campbell River   286-6166

*Carries other BC maps such as 1:20,000 TRIM maps. These and aerial photos are also available from:

Maps BC, 3rd Floor, 1802 Douglas Street, Victoria   387-1441

A compass is also useful, since even on a trail you can easily lose your way, especially in fog. At the least, a compass can keep you from going in circles. Remember, that though trails are in general well marked, they tend to become hard to follow or even erased in places by slides, periodic flooding or tree blowdowns.

The wise hiker travels with a friend in case of accident and leaves a trip plan, including time of return, with someone reliable. Extra food, even on day hikes, may come in handy. You should stay on trails unless absolutely sure where you are going. Be aware of the danger of being mistaken for a wild animal during hunting season, though hunting is not permitted within any of Vancouver Island's provincial parks. Good clothing, particularly strong footwear, is fundamental; waterproof matches, firestarter, maps, compass, a basic first aid kit, mosquito repellent and rainwear are essentials.

There is no one to pick up garbage so you must pack out all your paper, cans, etc. If you can, also take with you any other garbage left by thoughtless campers, especially bottles and cans. You will be helping greatly. There are no sanitary facilities provided in most areas away from roads so you should come prepared; a small shovel can be useful, and, if no fire hazard, burn your toilet paper because it does not decompose easily. An ice-axe is also a multi-use tool! Some areas are natural camping spots, and attract many people; if common sense and low impact camping techniques are not used these sites can be ruined for those who come later.

Don't expect trails to be well marked. As you go, glance back occasionally. Because the terrain often looks quite different when facing the other way, that will help you recognize features as you return. Plants grow slowly in alpine areas, and so places trampled by careless feet recover only slowly. It is best to stay on paths where these exist. Never roll rocks over cliffs - there might be someone below.

Please be careful and sparing with fires. Campfire-related activities such as off-trail wood collection, burn scars and incompletely-burned garbage make campfires the single most-damaging human impact on sensitive areas. In Strathcona Park's backcountry areas hikers are "encouraged" to use stoves, and forego campfires, in order to help protect the natural environment. In the Forbidden Plateau and Bedwell Lake (BC Parks) core areas this is now mandatory.

Thieves. Do not leave valuables in your car. Vehicles parked at a trailhead seem to be a target for thieves, who operate even during daytime. Many great hiking trips have been ruined as a consequence.

John W.E. Harris

CLUB ADDRESSES

For information on the following Vancouver Island Clubs:

- Outdoor Club of Victoria, (OCV)
- Alpine Club of Canada, Vancouver Island Section, (ACC)
- Comox District Mountaineering Club, (CDMC)
- Heathens Mountaineering Club (Campbell River), (HMC)
- Alberni Valley Outdoor Club, (AVOC)
- Island Mountain Ramblers (Nanaimo), (IMR)

Contact: The Federation of Mountain Clubs of BC
336, 1367 West Broadway, Vancouver, BC. V6H 4A9
Phone: (604) 737-3053

or The Outdoor Recreation Council of BC
334, 1367 West Broadway, Vancouver, BC. V6H 4A9
Phone: (604) 737-3058

Note: As of 1996, BC will have 2 area codes: 604 and 250.

OTHER USEFUL REFERENCES

BC Parks: Miracle/Strathcona   337-2400
1812 Miracle Beach Drive
Black Creek, BC. V9J 1K1

BC Forest Service
370 South Dogwood Street,   286-9300
Campbell River, BC. V9W 6Y7
or
P.O. Box 7000,   956-5000
Port McNeill, BC. V0N 2R0

Regional District of Comox/Strathcona   (Courtenay) 334-6000
4795 Headquarters Road   (Campbell River) 287-9612
P.O. Box 3370, Courtenay, BC. V9N 5N5

Regional District of Mount Waddington   956-3161
P.O. Box 729
Port McNeill, BC. V0N 2R0

Canadian Forest Products Ltd.   281-2300
Englewood Division, Woss

MacMillan Bloedel Ltd
Kelsey Bay Division, Sayward   282-3100
Eve River Division, Sayward   287-7473
Menzies Bay Division, Campbell River   287-5000

TimberWest Forest Ltd.
Campbell River   297-9181
Oyster River Division   287-7979

Western Forest Products Ltd.
Port McNeill   956-4446
Holberg   288-3362

Westmin Resources   287-9271
Myra Falls Operation
P.O. Box 8000
Campbell River, BC. V9W E52

Paradise Meadows

SECTION 1

ACCESS TRAILS/ROUTES INTO STRATHCONA PARK

NOTE: The following sub-sections describe in some detail these 36 access trails and routes. It is assumed that those travelling these routes, other than marked trails, are experienced hikers or climbers competent at map reading and route finding, and equipped with map, compass and altimeter. It is important that you read the section **"How To Use This Book"** *(page 6) before reading further.*

Off-road horse riding and bicycling is not allowed anywhere in Strathcona Park and a penalty fine is in place for violations.

TRAILS IN THE FORBIDDEN PLATEAU
AND COMOX GLACIER AREAS

Two public roads provide access to the Forbidden Plateau; namely, the roads to Wood Mountain Provincial Ski Park and Plateau Ski Lodge, and to Mount Washington Ski Resort. Access roads (other than MacBlo's road to Norm Lake used to access Gem Lake Trail) are administered by TimberWest Forest Ltd. who can provide you with their recreational leaflet. Extreme fire hazard may restrict access. The road up Cruickshank Canyon is washed out.

The Forbidden Plateau is a unique area and much has already been written about it. The trails there are long-established and offer opportunities for day or overnight hiking. For detailed information on the most regularly used trails shown on Maps D2 and E3 you should refer to BC Parks' new brochure. Signs on trees at intersections have been erected by the Comox District Mountaineering Club, and BC Parks has its official signing program.

Note: Should horse riders or mountain bikers be encountered off-road, hikers should consider that tourists may have unwittingly made a mistake, and inform them politely. Other abusers should be reported to BC Parks staff. Dogs must be on a leash at all times.

Remember that trails can become hard to follow in this alpine area and it is easy to take a wrong fork. When fog sets in trails can become confusing, and maps and compass will be essential.

Owing to increased recreational use and its resulting impacts in the Plateau area, low impact camping techniques are very important, with an emphasis on good sanitary habits and effective waste management. Take out **all** garbage.

Due to a concern that the Plateau's natural resources should not become depleted BC Parks has designated a "core area" within which campfires are not allowed and camping is restricted to specific, hardened sites. Camp stoves are now essential.

In the core area, camping is permitted only at Kwai Lake, Circlet Lake and Lake Helen Mackenzie, and these sites have pit toilets. Outside the core area there is camping at Douglas and McKenzie Lakes but no toilets, and BC Parks has no immediate plans to put any in.

Be prepared for a (core area) camping fee in 1996, probably in the order of $6 per tent per night.

Useful reference material includes:

BC Parks' brochures on Strathcona Park and Forbidden Plateau are regularly updated and include much useful information (addresses on page 9 and 11). These are available also at tourist information bureaus, and some sporting goods stores.

Map of "Comox Valley and Surrounding Area" (revised September, 1994) published by Comox Valley Search and Rescue Association, P.O. Box 3511, Courtenay, BC, V9N 6Z8 or at Mountain Meadows Sporting Goods store, Courtenay (see page 9).

(a) Boston Ridge Trail to Mount Becher (Map E3)

A good, circle day hike on marked trails: about 13 km. From Courtenay drive on public road almost to the Plateau Ski Lodge, about 24 km. You will find limited parking at start of trail (no longer signposted). The trail follows an old rail grade, crosses Boston Main logging road and Creek, then continues to the right, fairly steeply in places, up and over Boston Ridge and finally up to Mount Becher, with some marvellous views. From here either retrace your steps, or join the Becher Trail down to the Ski Lodge. The Boston Ridge Trail was constructed and flagged by CDMC.

(b) Paradise Meadows Access (Map D2)

Take the public road to Mount Washington. From Courtenay to the nordic ski parking lot and start of trail is about 26 km. The BC Parks pamphlet is very informative on the trails in the Forbidden Plateau.

(c) Paradise Meadows Loop (Map D2)

This trail starts at Mount Washington's nordic ski parking lot and runs down to the brown bridge on the old Battleship Lake Trail; then returns on the other side of Paradise Creek - length 2.2 km. It is a beautiful walk suitable for all ages.

(d) Sawdust Trail (Map D2)

Named informally by hikers because it is built up with wood chips, this 2.9 km trail from Paradise Meadows winds gently through rolling meadows to bring walkers of almost any ability level to Lake Helen Mackenzie. Following the lakeshore trail eastwards (ie. to the left) leads to the west side of Battleship Lake where you join the main trail back to Paradise Meadows. This pleasant loop requires about 3 hours, not including rest stops.

(e) Kwai Lake Loop Trail (Map D2)

At Lake Helen Mackenzie turn west to follow a rough but easy grade trail which ascends to subalpine meadows near the Park Rangers' cabin, and your first good views of Mount Albert Edward and Mount Regan. Turn left at Hairtrigger Lake and pass Kwai Lake on your left, a very beautiful and rewarding destination.

To return, follow signs to Croteau Lake, and from there to Battleship Lake. This 15 km loop requires a full day.

(f) Mount Albert Edward Trail/Route (Map D2)

From the Rangers' cabin (above) maintain your elevation to pass Hairtrigger Lake on your left. Another hour brings you to a short side trail leading to Circlet Lake. Camping at this popular location has heavily impacted the area, but it is a good place to stop before a steep climb onto the ridge leading to Albert Edward - especially with full packs. The trail becomes a route after the shoulder and tarns at 1,400 m. The summit is about 6 hours from the parking lot, one way. Many groups camp at Circlet Lake and travel light for a summit day-return (6 km and 4 hours one way). Remember to pack for a long day, and carry what you will need for exposed ridge travel and sudden weather changes.

(g) Gem Lake Trail (Map D2)

There is restricted access on the logging road up Oyster River to Norm Lake. A staffed security gate at Mile 16 ensures the road is closed to the public until 5 pm weekdays. It is open throughout weekends. Check with MacMillan Bloedel's office (see page 11) in Campbell River. From Norm Lake, a trail follows the grown-in road up to Gem Creek, then the west side of the creek to Gem Lake. Constructed and marked to Gem Lake by CDMC.

(h) Alone Mountain Trail (Map E4)

This makes a nice spring hike since the snow goes off the southern slope a few weeks earlier than on other mountains. Drive TimberWest's Comox Lake Main road to the top of the hill before you drop down to the Cruickshank River Bridge (about 25 km from Courtenay). A very short logging road leads in toward Alone Mountain. At its end drop down to the left, pick up the trail across the valley and follow it up to the top of Alone Mountain. In clear weather there are good views of Comox Glacier. The spring flowers are always beautiful and there are wild onions for nibbling. Trail was built and marked by CDMC.

(i) Sunrise Lake Route (Map D2)

You are recommended to pick up TimberWest's free map titled "Oyster River Operations". Just south of the Oyster River bridge turn off the Duncan Bay Main Line onto Oyster River Main. (Note: this is **not** the same road as MacMillan Bloedel's Oyster River Main on the other side of the river.) Head southwest for roughly 10 km and turn right onto Rossiter Main for 5 km to a bridge over Piggott Creek (Branch 151-5). After the bridge pass through a gate (locked on weekdays, but should be unlocked on weekends; check with TimberWest, and be careful not to get locked in when crews go home) and turn north across a bridge over Harris Creek. Stay on the west side of this creek to road's end (8 km) just west of the outfall of Harris Lake. Cross the creek to the start of the route.

(j) Idiens - Capes Lakes Route (Maps E4, D3 and D4)

Drive Comox Lake Main road to Cruickshank River [35] and take South Main for a short distance to a logging road leading up to the right. Park when it gets rough and hard to turn around. Walk up this logging road to large gully and turn left, following the road to its end. A flagged route starts here, goes up the centre of the ridge to open rock, turns left at the head of a ravine and follows the contour as far as a sign pointing to Idiens Lake, where there is good swimming in hot weather. Blazes lead to Idiens Lake memorial cairn. The route leads down to the outlet creek and around north side of Idiens Lake to Lee Plateau, where camping is possible and an excellent view of Comox Glacier is provided. Continue down to Capes Creek, avoiding the few cliffs. The Capes memorial cairn and plaque are just before the outfall of Capes Creek. From Capes Creek go roughly south up to Capes Ridge, from where you get the most magnificent view of Comox Glacier. Return via Capes Lake, branching right directly to Idiens - Capes Lakes junction and out the way you came in.

Even though the end of Capes Ridge shows on the map as being near South Main road, it is a precarious trip down, with huge belts of cliffs which are nearly impossible to avoid, and this method of return is definitely not recommended.

Ruth Masters

(k) Century Sam Lake Trail (Map D4)

This low-elevation trail starts just beyond the log crossing [36] for Comox Glacier Trail and goes up south side of Comox Creek to the lake and a nice little campsite. BC Parks cleared the trail of blowdown in 1995. Trail was made by CDMC in the 1960s.

(l) Comox Glacier /Route (Maps E4 and D4)

This trip is only for strong hikers, and should be made in reasonable weather, making a good 3-day hike: one day to the "frog pond" campsite, about 1.5 km along the ridge; a second day to travel light, up to the Glacier and back to camp; and a third day to pack out.

Road access to this area is subject to closures. Local conditions can be checked before you leave by calling BC Parks or TimberWest.

Access is by TimberWest logging roads for about 38 km from Courtenay. Roads are rough, and Datsio Creek bridge [34] has been pulled out and the stream bed re-established by Fisheries. The section from [34] to [36] on Maps D4 and E4 is suitable only for 4 wheel-drive with good clearance. Though some vehicles can still (1995) reach the trailhead, park cars at [34] and walk 2.5 km to start of trail. Go straight ahead on north side of creek about 300 metres. Cross on logs to a new section of trail with switchbacks. Unfortunately this only goes about a quarter of the way up and there is a lot of work to do to gain the ridge.

About a kilometre along the ridge there is a saddle which the hiker must negotiate. Descend from the ridge on the south side. It is steep and there is loose rock with quite a bit of exposure. From the saddle to the frog ponds is just a little further.

After the frog ponds, the trail reverts to a rough route and in places the rock steps can be quite intimidating, especially to tired hikers. This is a good place to use a rope for assurance, and you are advised to carry one (you should have one for the glacier anyway). Be cautious. There is also a lack of available water on this section.

There is a steep ascent to the 1240-m-level ridge leading to Black Cat Mountain (access ridge has fine views of Comox Glacier and of Century Sam Lake below). Follow along, up and over the north shoulder of Black Cat Mountain, down to Lone Tree Pass. Direct scramble from here up to south end of Comox Glacier. Cross wide flat snowfield to cairn. Get out if fog closes in, and be able to use map and compass to cross the glacier to the trail head.

Backpacking gear is essential, also maps and compass. Ice axes and rope are recommended, especially as crevasses are often hidden. Pack a stove along as firewood is getting scarce, and no-impact camping is a preferable goal. See connecting routes on Map D4 this book. The trail was built and marked by CDMC in the early 1960s.

(m) Kookjai Mountain Route, to Comox Glacier (Maps E5, E4 and D4)

Though a longer route to Comox Glacier, the Kookjai Mountain route crosses a lovely plateau area and avoids having to negotiate the exposed rock sections of the frog pond route.

Drive in from Courtenay as described above but turn southeast at the end of South Main towards Cougar Lake. Pull your vehicle off the road about 4-500 m north of where this rough logging road turns sharply east [46] on its way to Rough and Tumble Mountain. Heft your pack for an ascent of the obvious ridge to the west, perhaps skirting some bluffs at the 600-m level depending on the line you take. Follow the backbone of the ridge right up above the tree line. The going is good once you reach old growth timber, but before that you will have a "punishing" bush-bash of 2-3 hours.

Tatsno Lakes [47], is a very beautiful location with good tent sites and views. From here it is reasonable to make a day trip to Comox Glacier following a very defined system of ridges leading to Black Cat Mountain, where you join the Comox Glacier Route (above) at Lone Tree Pass. This makes for a very long day, so if you can go further on your first day you will shorten your second. A good (low impact) camp can be made at 1400 m up on the ridge top west of Tatsno Lakes where there are some small lakes. If you have more time, then Kwasson Lake is another good camping place along the way, with good access to clean water and perhaps less "buggy" than Tatsno Lakes.

OSHINOW LAKE AREA

This area constitutes the most southeasterly portion of Strathcona Park, and is heavily modified by logging. The south end of Oshinow Lake is accessed from Elsie Lake by a good-quality gravel road (which is suitable for 2-wheel-drive trucks) following the Ash River valley. Elsie Lake, in turn, is reached from Courtenay to the north by way of the Comox Lake Main logging road, and from Port Alberni to the southeast. Conditions on the roads are subject to change due to flooding, erosion and blowdown. Horses and mountain bikes are permitted on the old logging roads in this area.

(a) Upper Puntledge Route (Maps E5 and D4)

You will need a canoe for this. Drive on TimberWest Forest logging roads past the south end of Comox Lake to the foot of Willemar Lake. Paddle to the top end of Willemar and drag your canoe up the channel (about 200 m), or take a portage trail on the left ("right where you need it" says Ruth Masters, who helped put it in), and relaunch for a half-mile paddle through an "everglades" marshy area leading into Forbush Lake. There are two camping places: at the outlet, or at the top of the lake on the remains of the old cat-logging road which stopped at the Park boundary. Continue hiking on this old road, which has now softened into a pleasant trail, into the magnificent old growth forest of the Upper Puntledge. After about 2 km there is a delightful rest spot at a waterfall. From there on, the trail has been allowed to grow over, though it is a reasonable route through open timber all the way to Puntledge Lake. From here there are feasible route possibilities to Ash River and over to Drinkwater Creek, as well as connections to Margaret Lake and out by way of Price Creek.

(b) Oshinow Lake Access (Maps E5 and D5)

Camping and vehicle access is possible on the lake shore, at the end of the spur which roughly parallels the drainage into Oshinow Lake from Toy Lake. This is a feasible boat launch. The 5 km road on the northeast side of Oshinow Lake is not passable to vehicles, but is suitable for mountain bikes or hiking. This road bed may be removed in the near future as part of the Forest Renewal program.

(c) Toy, Junior and June Lakes Access (Map E5)

These small lakes are very close to a very rough dirt road, which is almost unsuitable for 4-wheel-drives. **June Lake** is adjacent to the road and two or three good entries exist for vehicles. At **Junior Lake** a small trail leads from a pull-off for 200 m to the lakeshore, and a short road goes right to **Toy Lake**. This road bed may be removed in the near future as part of the Forest Renewal program, and BC Parks may then join the lakes with a new trail.

About the V. I. T. I. S.

The Vancouver Island Trails Information Society is a non-profit society dedicated to providing accurate information to the public about trails and parks on Vancouver Island. Any profits made from the sale of its books are donated to like-minded worthy projects.

The society has its origins in the Outdoor Club of Victoria. O.C.V. members, especially Dr. Jim Fiddess and Ted Fairhurst, had long dreamed of producing a book about the trails known and used by their club. Their dreams came true in 1971 with the formation of a hard-working committee. The new editor was to be Jane Waddell, ably assisted by Bill Burroughs, John Harris, Dave Birch and Jane Toms among others.

The group incorporated as a non-profit society, the Outdoor Club of Victoria Trails Information Society, and produced its first book, HIKING TRAILS, Victoria and Southern Vancouver Island, in December of 1972. It proved to be an outstanding success, and by 1975 books on central and northern Vancouver Island had followed. Updated editions of each of these books are available. Hiking Trails I covers the Capital Regional District, and Hiking Trails II covers the Gulf Islands and the southeastern portion of Vancouver Island from Koksilah River Park to Mount Arrowsmith.

In 1993, in an effort to better describe the scope of its work, and to eliminate confusion, the society changed its name to the Vancouver Island Trails Information Society.

Della Falls

Photo: Bo Martin

DELLA FALLS TRAIL (Maps D5 And C5)

The Della Falls Trail leads hikers from the head of Great Central Lake to the base of the highest falls in Canada, a cascade from Della Lake. This 16 km trail, by way of Drinkwater Creek, is a long hike taking about 7 hours one way, and suitable for intermediate level hikers. The trail was originally built by Joe Drinkwater, a trapper, who also started the Ark Resort. Della Falls is named after his wife, and Margaret Lake, after Lady McBride.

For Great Central Lake drive 13 km west of Port Alberni on Highway 4 and instead of turning towards Sproat Lake go straight ahead on Great Central Lake Road for 8 km.

It takes 20 minutes to the Ark Resort, where you can park for a small fee and take a boat to Della Falls trailhead. Allow three days for a round trip if using a power boat, and six days by canoe.

A useful alternative if you have your own boat is to drive to another access road about halfway down the lake on the north side. For this approach, drive out on the Great Central Lake Road, and just before reaching the Ark Resort turn right onto a gravel road administered by MacMillan Bloedel Ltd., Ash Division (phone to check whether this road is open). After about 7 km turn left onto Ash Power Plant Road. About 1 km on, bear right, then after just under 5 km bear left downhill. After about another 4.5 km make two sharp lefts. The road continues about 1.5 km to an undeveloped camping area and the lakeshore. From here a trail, 2.5 km in length, follows up a wide valley to Lowry Lake where great fishing is to be found. From the lakeshore camping area, canoeing time to the head of the lake is about four or five hours.

The north and south shores of this narrow lake (about 33 km long) are very precipitous, so if canoeing, an early morning start is recommended. The lake is usually windswept by west winds in mid-afternoon and the water can be very rough with whitecaps. Watch for deadheads and standing dead trees along the shore, due to the raising of the lake level. Follow the shoreline despite the hazards, in case of rough water.

There are a few possible campsites about halfway along the north shore; those along the south shore are a little better.

Route Description:

Map D5

The trail starts at the lakehead's eastern shore where BC Parks has developed (1995) a campground with a bear-proof cache and a pit toilet. Along the trail, all the suspension bridges have been replaced with timber bridges. Much of the trail follows an old road bed left behind from logging and mining early in this century. The first 7 km follows a flat road bed through a mixed second growth forest to Margaret Creek. Once across the bridge at this creek the road bed continues through some old growth forest for 4 km, gently gaining elevation.

Map C5

Eleven km up the valley a new bridge over a nice gorge crosses Drinkwater Creek, and from there the trail continues more roughly to a bridge at 12.5 km. Beyond this bridge the roughest section of the trail passes through a rock slide which pushes you close to the creek. Gaining elevation again the road bed leads up to the Love Lake trail/Mount Septimus junction at about 15 km. The last kilometre to Della Falls emerges from open old growth forest into an avalanche run-out zone to the base of the Falls. Campfires are permitted but discouraged.

During the summers of 1983 and 1984 work crews improved the trail up to the Falls and built several bridges. In 1995 it was in good shape because BC Parks has concentrated on new bridge construction. Check maps C5 and D5 for campsites and toilets (toilet paper is not supplied). Camping is good on the north side of Drinkwater Creek about 1 km below the Falls, which are visible from the campsite. These well-known falls are in three successive drops, each about 150 m. A climb to the top of the falls is possible but a little dangerous.

There is much evidence of the extensive mining activity in this area. Please do not remove or destroy any remaining mining equipment which now forms part of the historical record.

(a) To Della Lake

A difficult and dangerous marked route leads up the cliffs to the south of the falls. In 1991, Parks staff removed the cables which were hung on this route. To get there cross the Drinkwater Creek on the main bridge just above the upper camp. Walk 100 m and look for a trail to the left. The correct trail/route to Della Lake crosses a single beam bridge 25 m after leaving trail to the falls. It travels up through dense bush to the base of cliffs and then follows obvious lines up through steep mixed ground. Above 800 m it leads up and right [44], through bush, and connects to a ledge. This ledge leads up cliffs and straightforward ramps to Della Lake, which is in a spectacular setting of rugged mountain peaks.

(b) To Love Lake

Our map shows the switchbacking trail starting by the old sawmill, which goes up to Love Lake. Turn uphill at the sign "Love Lake/Mount Septimus". This is now a well-built trail and a pleasant hike to good (best at 1200-m level) views of Della Falls. Trail switchbacks steeply. At the 1220-m level break off to the right and pick up the trail to Love Lake. On the way in, camping is also possible on the Drinkwater Creek gravel bar about 2 km before reaching the Love Lake turn-off, but **beware of suddenly-rising waters.**

See also Section 2, routes (c), page 50, and (j), page 62.

NOTES: The Ark Resort's mailing address is Site 306, C1, RR#3, Great Central Lake Road, Port Alberni, BC V9Y 7L7 (phone 723-2657) . The resort also rents out canoes and power boats, and operates a water taxi service which will drop you off (takes an hour from the resort to the trailhead) and pick you up again on a pre-arranged date. Ask for their Della Falls special rate, which is (1995) a four-day canoe rental for $60/person or a three-day power boat rental for the same price plus fuel. You can camp at the Ark Resort: they have 20 campsites for $17/night (and 9 RV sites). Alternatively, a 3-seater float plane from Courtenay to the trailhead will cost (1995) about $156 one-way.

BEDWELL RIVER (OINIMITIS) TRAIL (Maps B6, B5 and C5)

The Bedwell River, formerly called the Bear River, was the traditional home of the Oinimitis (meaning "bear") people, who, in the fall, would gather at the delta to fish and hunt. In 1865, John Buttle travelled up this river, climbing an unnamed mountain near Ursus Creek. He was soon followed by placer miners who swarmed here on the rumour of gold. Mining has continued in this valley since that time, and in 1962 the lower valley was partially logged. In the winter of 1994/95 the first 2 km of the old logging road were re-opened and an area of privately-owned timber was clearcut. The valley has been deleted from, and returned to, Strathcona Park since 1986. The Oinimitis Trail was built by the Friends of Strathcona to provide access to this remote and delightful valley.

Approach. From Tofino, boat or air transportation is needed to reach the head of Bedwell Sound, approximately 32 km (20 miles). If travelling by sea kayak or canoe this trip will take about a day and a half. Power boat transportation can be arranged through The Whale Centre in Tofino and the trip takes about one and a half hours.

Trail Head. There is an obvious, open flat area by the logging bridge with good camping, but fill up your water jugs on the way up the Sound because there is no fresh water close by.

Map B6

Trail Description. From the landing area, follow the obvious, recently-rebuilt logging road north, through 2 km of fresh clearcut, to reach the first camping site and fresh water. From this point the trail follows the banks of the Bedwell and there are good views of Ursus Mountain. One km farther on cross Cotter Creek and a little farther, just past Penny Creek, a small trail to the right leads to Walter Guppy's cabin by the river (about 4 km from tidewater). This is a good shelter in bad weather.

As you continue on the main trail, which now begins to climb a little, you reach the "3-Mile" log-crossing [40], where the trail crosses above a gorge on the Bedwell. Here a fine new suspension bridge has been constructed by the Friends of Strathcona.

26

In August, 1994, the Friends of Strathcona dedicated this bridge to Gayle McGee, a departed Friend and enviro/activist.

One kilometre farther on you reach the boundary of Strathcona Park, which is not marked. The trail now opens up and stays well above the main river-canyon. There are beautiful deep pools and water-carved rocks where the river bends (well below the trail), and a fine view of Mariner Mountain.

After the rock-cut, the trail becomes narrower, and after 500 m leads you to a rocky washout which can be crossed using the remains of an old bridge. Shortly after this the Bedwell is again crossed by a good bridge, although this is well overgrown, above a narrow canyon where the river roars far below. An interesting viewing point!

Map B5

Approximately 800 m farther on, several flagging tapes on the left mark the beginning of the difficult route [41] to Mariner Mountain. This route is quite steep, and should only be attempted by experienced mountaineers because ropes and ice axes are required.

Noble Creek is 200 m past this side trail, and 1 km past this creek there is an interesting side trip to see the "Twin Falls" and canyon. Small cairns on the right mark an easy bushwhack to this viewpoint.

Four km from Noble Creek the trail is forced closer to the river by big cliffs and crosses the river again (and for the last time) at Ashwood Creek [42]. This can be tricky, since you have to ford the river. Once you are across, a spacious campsite can be found 5-10 minutes walk up the trail along a dry creek bed that leads off to the left. This fine gravel bar campsite has an open view of the whole valley and Big Interior Mountain. The average hiker should reach this spot, about 14 km from tidewater, in about 5-8 hours.

Map C5

Continuing on from Ashwood Creek the trail swings away from the river for 1.5 km and then bypasses a 100 m washed-out section before rejoining the main road again. Another kilometre brings you to the You Creek bridge [43] which is badly decayed. Care must be taken to avoid the rotten and unstable parts of this crossing.

The old road continues for another 2 km up the valley, as it swings north and begins to climb more steeply. At the end of the old logging road the trail follows a dry creek bed for a short section before turning off to the right (look for flagging tape) to reach the old growth forest. A series of old game trails, climbing steeply in sections, brings you onto a slide area by way of a small river crossing. Cairns mark the route across, climbing a bit to again reach the old growth trees. The trail can easily be picked up here, winding through forest and swampy areas.

Shortly before K2 Creek a small side trail leads to an impressive waterfall, unofficially named "Doran Falls" after two brothers, Stan and George Doran, who rebuilt this section of trail when well into their 70s. A rustic bridge atop a waterfall leads over K2 Creek. Climbing up you will soon reach Oinimitis Lake (by a side trail) and in half an hour, through fragile alpine meadows, Bedwell Lake. BC Parks' trail starts at the campsite at the southeast corner of the lake.

Linked with the BC Parks trail constructed from Thelwood Creek to Bedwell Lake, a through trip from Bedwell Sound to Bedwell Lake will take 2-3 days (16-20 hours), with a further day (2-4 hours) to reach Jim Mitchell Lake road.

A further choice can be made at Bedwell Lake, either to follow a route to the Price Creek trail via Cream Lake (14 km of difficult terrain taking 1-2 days, see route (c) in Section 2, page 50), or to go via the Drinkwater Creek valley to Della Falls and Great Central Lake (boat needed).

WESTMIN RESOURCES MINE AREA

Access by road is 13 km from Ralph River campground to the minesite. Continue on road past the mine to the tourist parking lot. Cars may be parked here for the duration of the hike, but no camping is permitted in or around the parking lot.

Up to 4:00 pm, Westmin Resources Ltd. may be reached at 287-9271. Hikers may use the recreation building pay phone to arrange to be picked up. In the case of an emergency the company office will help contact authorities to arrange helicopter evacuation.

(a) Phillips Ridge Trail (Map C4)

This well-constructed trail affords access to the high ridge tour of the Phillips Ridge watershed without the need to cross Buttle Lake by boat. Drive through the mine site to a car park, then walk about 30 m past the yellow gate on gravel road and turn right at the BC Parks sign. The trail starts at the 360 m level and switchbacks up to the 1300 m level. It passes through open woods up to Arnica Lake and then enters alpine meadows and ridges.

BC Parks staff have been making many improvements to the Arnica Lake area, which, as a popular destination, was showing some wear and tear. Hikers are now directed around the east side of the lake only, and the old camp and trails are now a reclamation area. Fire pits have been eradicated. Five tent platforms have been installed at a dedicated campsite and a boardwalk provides lakeshore access. In the summer of 1996, BC Parks will install a pit toilet and a bear-proof cache at the northeast side of the lake, not far from the campsite.

In order to help protect this area from unintentional abuse, BC Parks has erected an educational sign describing ethics for backcountry users.

Hiking time to Arnica Lake, 3 to 4 hours; with large packs, 4 to 5 hours. First available water is at 460 m, a few minutes past waterfalls; second water at 730 m; next at Arnica Lake, 1300 m. Areas around the lake and the shoulders of Mount Phillips have beautiful flowers in season. A fairly strenuous day hike. See also Section 2, route (f), page 58.

This trail was initiated by Don Apps of the Comox District Mountaineering Club (CDMC) and has been a joint project of BC Parks and the Federation of Mountain Clubs of BC with work being done mainly by CDMC and Island Mountain Ramblers (IMR) volunteers.

(b) Upper Myra Falls Trail (Maps C4 and B4)

Having parked as above, walk past gate on gravel road about 800 metres to where the trail cuts into the bank on the right side. Follow the markers (placed by CDMC). This is a nice valley walk on a fair trail through mature trees. There is one creek crossing on a new bridge. At the end of the trail by the falls, BC Parks has built a lookout platform. Time - 1 hour each way.

As part of the Adopt-A-Trail program organized by the Federation of Mountain Clubs of BC, this trail and its maintenance was formally adopted in 1991 by the CDMC. This was the first Adopt-A-Trail project on Vancouver Island.

(c) Mount Thelwood area from Myra Creek (Maps C4 and B4)

As above, follow the Upper Myra Falls trail for about $1/2$ hour. Just past an area of blowdown the trail turns southwards, downhill, to a fork in the creek. Creek crossing can be difficult during the spring when water levels are high. From here the route is sparsely flagged to the centre of the ridge, and follows the ridge as a bush-whack. This flagged (once upon a time) route (marked by CDMC) gives easy and short access to the Thelwood area. During summer there can be a serious problem finding water. The ridge itself is dry, and it is a long way from Myra Creek to alpine areas where water may be found. Be sure to carry sufficient amounts of water. See also the relevant paragraph of route (d), on page 53.

(d) Westmin to Tennent Lake to Mount Myra (Map C4)

From the power house above the minesite follow the penstock road up to Tennent Lake (very rough and steep). Turn south near the lakeshore and look for flagging tape markers. The route (rough, with many windfalls) leads around to the east side of the ridge and terminates at a rock slope (not too steep). Above is a semi-alpine area on the northwest ridge; easy to follow the ridge up to summit. For route from Mount Myra to the Mount Thelwood area see also Section 2, route (i), page 61.

BUTTLE LAKE TRAILS

Buttle Lake is a long (20 km) narrow lake running north-south and providing very important marine and road access into the central area of Strathcona Park. The paved road which follows the east shore leaves the Gold River Road (Highway 28) at Buttle Narrows and terminates at Westmin Mine.

(a) Lupin Falls Nature Walk (not shown on our maps)

About 8 km south of Buttle Lake bridge find this trail signposted by BC Parks. A 20-minute loop nature walk through open "big tree" forest brings you to Lupin Falls. On the lake side there are some picnic tables and walking access to the beach.

(b) Jack's Augerpoint Trail (Map C3)

The start is located off the Buttle Lake Parkway about 20.5 km south of the Highway 28 junction, or if going north from Karst Creek boat ramp, 2.4 km. Side-of-road parking. The old Augerpoint Trail was burned out in a forest fire and is currently unusable, but Jack Shark (a member of CDMC) has constructed a trail which goes up north of the burn. The start of this unofficial trail is 550 m north of the old trail and is flagged, but not signposted except for a red line on the highway. It is narrow and steep at times and there are several hazardous spots. In about two hours you reach a little pond where you can camp, and three hours later, at the 1400-m level, the trail breaks out into the sub-alpine of a pleasant plateau with small ponds and good camping opportunities. The trail turns south for a half mile to link up with the old trail, and this section has now been slashed out and marked.

If travelling west from Ruth Masters Lake, do not go down the old trail to Buttle Lake, which seems nice at the start but will drop you into the ghastly burned area. Continue north for one kilometre to an area of small ponds (good camping) and descend from there on a steep trail. See also the Augerpoint route, Section 2 (h), page 61.

(c) Augerpoint Fire Trail

This trail, suitable for all ages, is a 15 - 20 minute walk through an area burned during the Augerpoint fire. The trail starts from the picnic area.

(d) Karst Creek Trail

The trail, suitable for all ages, is signposted at the Karst Creek day area where there is swimming, a boat ramp and picnicking. The creek disappears into limestone, and the 45-minute loop trail returns along the beautiful valley floor. (The boat ramp here used to be called the Ralph River Boat Ramp).

(e) Shepherd Creek Loop Trail (Map C3)

The trailhead is directly across the highway from BC Parks Ralph River campground, and provides an interesting 1-km nature walk featuring a Pacific dogwood tree and a marshy area. For its first 200 m the trail follows the bank of the creek, and overall has an elevation gain of 50 m.

(f) Shepherd Creek Route (Maps C4 and C3)

Hikers on the high ridges east of Buttle Lake have few routes to follow when escaping bad weather. This rescue trail was worked on by hiking club volunteers in order to provide some help to those trying to drop down to Buttle Lake and the highway.

(g) Lower Myra Falls Trail (Map C4)

One kilometre beyond Thelwood bridge at the south end of Buttle Lake (and 1 km from the end of the paved road) turn onto a gravel road leading to a signed parking area, and follow a gentle walking trail down to Myra Creek Falls. The trail is suitable for day trippers. This 1-km walk takes 20-40 minutes and features old growth forest and a good view of these impressive multiple falls.

(h) Marble Meadows Trail (Map C3)

From Buttle Lake bridge drive south about 23 km to Karst Creek boat ramp if using a boat, or to the Augerpoint Rest Spot if using a canoe. When landing at BC Parks' Marine Site at Phillips Creek watch for underwater stumps. The trail starts on the north side of the creek and is well-graded to a creek and camping spot half-way.

The trail then becomes steeper up to alpine meadows. This trail was constructed as a Centennial project by IMR and CDMC with the help of BC Parks. Time up to the Wheaton Hut area is about 5 hours (some groups with heavy packs require 7 hours). This hut is very small (and usually filthy) and the biffy is gone. Hikers should depend on using tents. See also Section 2, route (f), page 58.

(i) Flower Ridge Trail (Maps C4 and C5)

This trail is steep, rough and there is a lack of water. It is not recommended for novices. The trailhead is about 3 km south of Ralph River campsite (signposted by Henshaw Creek). Elevation gain up to the ridge is about 1160 m, over about 6 km. Time up, 4 or 5 hours; down, 2½ to 3 hours. The first part of the trail is well-defined through beautiful, open woods. Although steep in places because the trail lacks switchbacks, there are some level and downhill sections. After the first hour there are two or three side trails which lead to viewpoints overlooking Buttle Lake and the mountains. Further up, a burn area affords good views of Mount Myra. This can make a good day hike. To reach the alpine area at the top of the ridge where you get the best views, and there are some nice ponds to camp by, you should allow plenty of daylight hours. See also Section 2, routes (b), page 48, and (c), page 50.

(j) Price Creek Trail (Maps C4 and C5)

Recommended for strong hikers, the trail gains 1200 m of elevation over 8½ km and takes about 7 hours one way. Members of the CDMC have relocated the upper part of this old elk trail which provides good access to Cream Lake. The trail stays on the east side of Price Creek right up to the Cream Creek junction. Here a log crosses Price Creek (with hand cable). The trail continues on the north side of Cream Creek to about 275 m below Cream Lake, then crosses an open slide area up above the east side of the creek. This trail now avoids the worst of the rock slide areas but the upper part is a very steep chute.

See also Section 2, routes (c), page 50, and (j), page 62.

(k) Thelwood Lake Route (Maps C4 and C5)

At the head of Buttle Lake, drive on Westmin roads to the parking lot at the start of the Bedwell Lake Trail. Access from here to Jim Mitchell Lake (flooded 1985) is made either on foot or by 4-wheel-drive vehicle only. The old connecting road to the Price Creek access road (which appears on the federal NTS map) is washed out and will not be restored. Camping is not permitted at or near the dam. These roads will not be ploughed in winter.

Currently, 1995, there is no easy access from Jim Mitchell Lake dam to the Thelwood Lake area. It is advisable to take a canoe to the head of Jim Mitchell Lake then hike a rough bush route (made by Westmin) on the south side of the creek to Thelwood Lake.

(l) Bedwell Lake Trail (Maps C4 and C5)

BC Parks has developed the Bedwell Lake Trail as an opportunity for less-experienced hikers to access an alpine/subalpine area, especially on a day-use basis. This trail links with the Bedwell River Trail to form a through route between the Pacific Ocean (at Bedwell Bay) and Buttle Lake.

The use of steel stairways on this trail continues to offend some hikers while being appreciated by others. This trail is now extremely popular and a significant impact on a sensitive and fragile area is the result. Visitors to the area can protect the wilderness qualities of this beautiful area by practising low impact techniques. One of the best ways to see this area without further impacting it is to visit as a day hiker. With just a day pack, the trail will flow beneath your feet and you will gain elevation without stress.

There are many black bears in this area, and a management concept is being developed to prevent bear habitat from being disturbed by visitors. You will help by only camping in designated areas. Perhaps this background will help you, as you walk this trail, to think about the difficulties of managing recreation use in wilderness areas.

Access the trailhead from the south end of Buttle Lake, leaving the Buttle Lake Parkway as if for Jim Mitchell Lake (Map C4), following signs for the trailhead 6.8 km up a rough 2-wheel-drive road to an information shelter and parking at the trailhead.

Due to a concern that the Bedwell Lake area's natural resources should not become depleted, BC Parks has designated this as a "core area" within which campfires are not allowed and camping is restricted to specific, hardened sites. Camp stoves are now essential.

The trail is 6 km long, gains 600 metres in elevation, and takes about 3 hours. It ascends a steep forested valley with numerous bridge crossings and breaks out into a hilly subalpine area with two lakes and many tarns and creeks.

As shown on Map C5: there is designated camping at Baby Bedwell Lake, with six tent platforms and pit toilet, and on the east shore of Bedwell Lake [15] where there are ten tent platforms and a toilet.

Note: It will be obvious to experienced campers that this kind of environment is very susceptible to the impacts of human use. At this altitude plants have a very short growing season and cannot recover from trampling. Soil cover in the alpine is thin and easily washed away if it is disturbed, for example, by trenching around tent sites. Wood is scarce, and, even outside the core area, campfires are now discouraged simply to preserve this natural resource. Restrict your hiking to marked trails. Use the toilets, not the bushes, and wash well away from the lake so your wash water filters through the ground.

The Bedwell Trail is becoming a popular way to reach Cream Lake, and the route between Bedwell and Cream lakes is described in Section 2, end of part (c), page 51. It takes 1 to 3 hours, one way.

Other side trips from Bedwell Lake include hikes up Mount Tom Taylor and Big Interior Mountain, each requiring a full day.

See Section 2, route (d), page 52, for the route from Bedwell Lake to Burman Lake.

TRAILS FROM HIGHWAY 28 (GOLD RIVER ROAD)
(a) Elk River Trail south to Elk River Pass (Maps A1 and A2)

From the bridge at Buttle Narrows drive about 23 km on Highway 28, and find sign to Elk River Trail just before Drum Lakes. Driving time from Campbell River is about 1 hour. Follow signs to start of trail. BC Parks has relocated the start of the trail and also built a new parking lot. The new trail creates an unnecessary climb and descent which is not appreciated by hikers just starting out with heavy packs. Old hands prefer the original trail start located closer to the river.

The trail is essentially an old elk trail which has been improved over the years, first by a government crew, then by some members of the IMR and CDMC, and more recently by BC Parks, who have cleared the trail nicely up to the gravel flats below Landslide Lake and upper river flats. It is now quite a good trail and hazardous log crossings at Butterwort, Volcano and Puzzle Creeks have been replaced by sturdy bridges built by the Island Mountain Ramblers in conjunction with BC Parks.

Due to the popularity of this trail, BC Parks is having to develop management strategies to protect the area from the effects of human use, and abuse. This includes concentrating tent camping at sites which can take the impact, and these locations are shown on Maps A1 and A2. Waste management is a high priority and BC Parks has provided pit toilets at these sites. Elsewhere, defecate in the bush well away from streams. Carry a plastic trowel so you can dig a small scat hole, and either flame your toilet paper or pack it out with you in a plastic bag (because it won't decompose). This is important.

At Volcano Creek there have been numerous bear sightings. It is about a 3 hour hike for a hiker with full overnight gear to the Butterwort Creek gravel bar, and about 6 hours to the gravel flats. From here one can make day excursions, especially to Landslide Lake. See also Section 2, routes (e), page 57, and (k), page 62.

During the strong earthquake of June 24, 1946, a part of Mount Colonel Foster fell away into the lake below, now officially named Landslide Lake. The water was displaced so violently that it caused havoc in this part of the valley taking out hundreds of trees, down to bedrock, for about 800 metres. This scar is clearly visible. See photograph, page 42.

To Landslide Lake.

Though part of a main route to the Golden Hinde (3-4 days one way) the Elk River Trail is used mostly by those who want to hike in to Landslide Lake. They camp en route and take a daypack on the second day, either camping a second night or heading out. Note: camping at Landslide Lake is not allowed.

At about 9.5 km a side trail to Landslide Lake leaves the Elk River Trail (map A2) after it crosses the outfall stream where BC Parks has installed a new bridge. A newly-constructed trail climbs to the side of a waterfall (very impressive in flood) and leads to Landslide Lake. For those en route to the Golden Hinde this makes a pleasant lunch break provided backpacks are stashed and not carried up to the lake then down again.

(b) Crest Mountain Trail (Map A1)

Crest Creek Crags has become a very popular rockclimbing area. However, non-designated camping within one kilometre of a highway is not allowed in BC's provincial parks, so you are advised not to camp here. This area is closely monitored by Parks staff.

From Buttle Lake bridge on Highway 28 drive to Drum Narrows, about 24 km. Signposted and some parking. Cross the Narrows by bridge onto the trail which is clearly defined and graded at the lower levels. It was originally constructed by the BC Forest Service for a study of climatic conditions, but as it is no longer used for this purpose the trail has deteriorated higher up. At the 550-m level a tree has been felled to cross the creek, but it is not always needed. Beyond this level the trail becomes steep, but even those who do not go up the whole way will find there are some fine viewpoints.

Time up to 1440-m level and an alpine lake - about 4 hours. Allow time to continue another kilometre to the rounded top and to explore the ridge northwards. This alpine area is a continuation of the alpine mountain ridges, but is not part of the interconnecting route system previously described. On good days there are spectacular views in all directions, especially south across the valley towards Kings Peak, Elkhorn Mountain and Mount Colonel Foster.

(c) Kings Peak access route (Map A1)

A new trailhead has been established. Driving west from Buttle Lake turn left on the Elk River Timber (ERT) logging road (just after the highway passes under a power transmission line). One km later, park at a pull-out on the left before the logging road crosses the Elk River. Just beyond the power line clearing, the new trail leads up, crossing a small creek and joining the access route on the other side. A new bridge was placed here in late 1995.

An alternative is to drive a dirt road under the powerline and link up with the standard route as shown on the map. This trail is steep in sections and most groups with full pack will take 5-6 hours to reach the upper bowl. In the spring, caution is required where the trail opens into a curved gulley just below the bowl. Avalanches can funnel into the gulley, from which hikers have no fast exit.

During summer or even late spring the snow gulley between Kings Peak and a lower summit to the west (known locally and incorrectly as Queens Peak) will not be a safe option. Instead, cross the bowl westwards to gain the ridge to Queens Peak. This is a safer route anyway. Be prepared to be offended by the presence of a radio repeater cone on the summit of Kings Peak.

This route has been adopted by The Heathens Mountaineering Club. (Note: the name of this club refers to those who prefer "the heath", or the high areas where the heather grows, and not necessarily to the philosophical beliefs of the members.)

DONNER LAKE ACCESS

Donner Lake is a popular fishing destination, and a canoe/hiking access route into the park mountains. Float planes are no longer allowed to use this lake. It is accessed by old logging roads, which are in poor condition and sometimes washed out. The area reached by the road seems to be used by the 4-wheel-drive party crowd, and you should be cautious about leaving your vehicle, or camping overnight, until BC Parks upgrades the road access, the facilities and their supervision.

In the town of Gold River, heading west, take the second left turn after the arena entrance, onto a paved road (Ucona Main) signed "To the Re-cycling Plant". Stay on this road (now dirt) for 12 km to Star Lake. Three km past the lake take the first left turn (U7). Next turn right onto PFP road to Kunlin Lake, and (now 4-wheel-drive is needed) drive around the lake to Donner Falls. Park here and walk up beside the river to Donner Lake.

GOLD LAKE TRAILS

There are two routes (three, including air access by float plane) into Gold Lake.

From the east :

On Highway 19 from Campbell River drive north about 14.5 km to Menzies Bay Division, MacMillan Bloedel Ltd. Office is open 7:30 am to 4 pm, Monday to Friday. Check conditions if hike is planned early in year. For detailed information ask for Menzies Bay Division guide map. All roads are open except spurs with active logging. Access may not be possible in extreme fire hazard weather. Observe all signs. Turn left onto Salmon River Main road at the company's workshop and drive 30 km to the start of trail (signposted) at Spur H. Limited parking. From Spur H.1, only 4-wheel-drive vehicles can proceed farther. Time: 2 hours for the 5-km walk in.

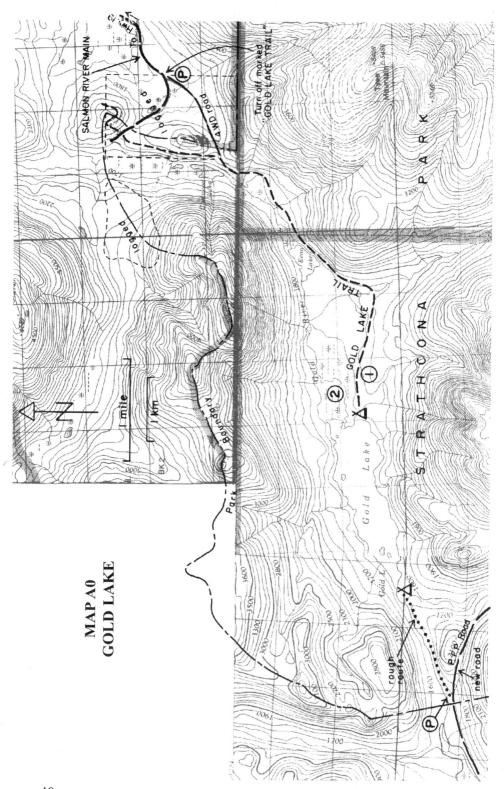

MAP A0
GOLD LAKE

40

All streams flood and some are impassable when rain is heavy. Snowfall in this area is heavy and the snowpack holds into late June. West of Eena Lake the trail goes through a gravel area and if the water is high the creek may be crossed by a log. The marshy area [1] can only be crossed in dry weather. Camp on the gravel bar [2] (but watch for rain flooding the river), or use old campsites on the south bank.

The trail was built by the Campbell River Wildlife Association in 1970 and is signposted by the BC Forest Service.

From the west:

Pacific Forest Products has opened access to the west side of Gold Lake with the construction of a logging road (usually 2-wheel drive) which passes through the northwest corner of the park to access timber outside the park boundary.

This can be reached from Gold River by following the Gold River Main logging road (north) as far as the Muchalat River bridge. Turn right and follow East Main (keeping right at the Y junction) for 30 km to enter the park.

The parking lot is on the left side of the road, and the trail may be difficult to find if it is overgrown with bush. The trail is in poor condition but the distance to Gold Lake is only 2-3 km.

STRATHCONA PARK LODGE

Located on the eastern shore of Upper Campbell Lake, 40 km west of Campbell River on Highway 28 to Gold River and 6 km before the road enters Strathcona Park, this internationally-known outdoor recreation center is well-situated for visitors to this part of the park.

The Lodge offers good-quality meals and accommodation, and a year-round program for all ages. Instructional courses range from nature walks and canoe camping to white water kayaking, rockclimbing and west coast explorations.

For more information, and free brochure, phone: (604) 286-3122.

Landslide Lake and Mount Colonel Foster

SECTION 2

THE BACKCOUNTRY ROUTES OF STRATHCONA PARK

NOTE: The following sub-sections describe in some detail a selection of backcountry routes in Strathcona Park. It is assumed that those travelling these routes are experienced hikers or climbers competent at map reading and route finding, and equipped with map, compass and altimeter. It is important that you read the section "How To Use This Book" (page 6) before reading further.

Off-road horse riding and bicycling is not allowed anywhere in Strathcona Park and a penalty fine is in place for violations.

It is with some misgiving that we publish these details, as the alpine and sub-alpine areas, through which these routes go, are easily damaged irreparably by over-use and, above all, by thoughtless camping practices. With society's growing awareness of a need to preserve some of the outdoors in its natural state, it is to be hoped that considerate visitors will use Strathcona Park without ruining the very landscape they came to enjoy.

A special feature of Strathcona Park is the way high alpine ridges interconnect, enabling long traverses and circular tours of the Park to be made mostly above tree line.

This section of the book takes the form of a route description for an extended backpacking trip that, by following the system of interconnecting ridges, takes us right through Strathcona Park from east to south and then west to north. In reality, such a trip is possible and would take about three weeks, though re-supplies of food would be a logistical challenge.

Starting from Mount Becher in the Forbidden Plateau section of the Park, the ridges are followed southwards to Comox Glacier, then west to Mount Septimus and Big Interior Mountain, north to Mount Thelwood, thence following the height of land to Burman Lake, passing south of the Golden Hinde and continuing in a northwesterly direction on the height of land and down to the Elk River valley. This route is almost entirely in alpine parkland or high alpine, only dropping into the timber for two short sections through its entire length.

Most hikers will hike this route a section at a time, so the text is divided into sections which can be used as needed. The maps in this book show the access points to this high level route, and for access trail descriptions see Section 1.

In addition, this section of the book describes other high-level routes which can be enjoyed individually or in combination, including a number of loop routes which return you to where (or almost where) you started. For example, four such trips, each of about a week's duration, may be made from Buttle Lake.

Probably the most popular, and the easiest, circular tour is that which starts and ends at Phillips Creek, traversing the entire Phillips Creek watershed boundary by way of the high divide, and including Marble Meadows in the route. It is, of course, necessary to cross the lake by boat to reach Phillips Creek.[i]

Another tour follows the trail from Buttle Lake to Augerpoint, and circles the Ralph River watershed, arriving back at Ralph River campground, about 5 km south of the starting point. Then, starting from Ralph River campsite, you can follow ridges around the Shepherd Creek watershed and back to starting point. The last and shortest of this quartet, also starting from Ralph River, circles the Henshaw Creek watershed and includes the Flower Ridge Trail.

A weather caution. Those who travel in high areas should always keep a careful watch for changes in the weather, for even in summer a major storm of 2 or 3 days duration can occur, and it can be quite cold, with high winds in exposed areas. A big storm usually takes at least half a day to get started, so those who get caught unawares have generally themselves to blame. If one seems to be

---

[i] Note: It is possible to make the same tour starting and ending at Westmin Resources minesite, using the Phillips Ridge access trail and thus avoiding the need for a boat. It means, however, that you have to hike up to alpine not once but twice, each time a 6 hour climb with a full pack.

blowing up, stop at a good campsite, even as early in the day as noon, for in such circumstances it is better to camp early than to press on until late in the day, when, cold, wet and tired, you may have to settle for an indifferent spot.

When seeking a campsite for bad weather it may be best to drop down from the alpine terrain 300 metres or so into the timber, preferably on south or west facing slopes, where Douglas-fir is found at higher elevation than it is on slopes facing north and east. Here one may camp with good shelter and, if necessary, make a fire without damaging the alpine terrain. Old Douglas-fir bark makes a perfect substitute for coal and maintains a warm glowing fire for hours. When the weather improves, an hour's hike or so will have you back on the ridges and the detour will have been well worthwhile for the extra comfort it provided while the storm raged.

When travelling in the timber, full use should be made of game trails. Deer and elk trails often are the best routes along valley floors and up the timbered ridges to the alpine zone. Avoid the bottoms of V-shaped valleys and make for the ridges instead. Flat-bottomed valleys often have good game trails beside the creek or on a flat bench 30 metres or so above it.

When choosing a route for approaching an unfamiliar mountain, remember that unlogged ridges are generally better going than valleys or draws and that, in central Vancouver Island, south and west facing slopes below 1230 m are less bushy than those facing north and east. Above this level the reverse is true. Douglas-fir forest is clearer to walk through than cedar and hemlock. From afar you can tell cedar from fir by its yellower green. Avoid a slope with many dead trees; their bare branches let the light in and make it bushy underfoot.

Going up a mountain, all the ridges converge towards the summit, which is consequently hard to miss. But coming down, it is very easy in cloud to pick the wrong ridge, and perhaps come down in the wrong valley. An altimeter is a worthwhile addition to the essential map and compass, for on the descent, when the ridge suddenly divides, a knowledge of your altitude should enable you to pinpoint your position accurately and pick the right route. If you went up in clear weather and are coming down in cloud, it all looks so different that every landmark you noticed and remembered from the ascent will be appreciated. Remember that if the weather is worsening the barometer is probably falling and the altimeter will probably read high. A change of one kilopascal in barometric pressure represents about 90 m error in altitude (or, a change of 1/4" of mercury represents an error of about 250 ft. in altitude).

(a) Mount Albert Edward to Comox Glacier (Maps D2, D3, D4)

This is one tough trip, and it follows rocky barren ridges which provide few sheltered spots able to accommodate more than a couple of tents. However, there is a rugged beauty to the route, especially if you appreciate interesting rocks.

Map D3

This route leaves the main route up Albert Edward at the 1880-m level, where the former turns west. If you have already had a full day you may need to camp at one of the small lakes here [ii].

Follow the height of land south, up the north side of Mount Frink (the 1960-m ridge west of Castlecrag, go left around the summit rocks and down the centre of the west ridge. Don't turn south too soon or you will run into cliffs. At about the 1600-m level [1] above the steep section east of Charity Lake, turn south and follow ledges back to regain the centre of the ridge at about the 1540-m level, then down the ridge to a good campsite just below the col between Faith Lake and Charity Lake (time - about 5 hours from start).

Map D3

For the route around the north peak of Mount George V, follow open areas up to about the 1630-m level, then contour west across the mountain's north snowfield. At the steep drop-off on the west ridge turn sharp left [2] and follow up this well-defined ridge to about 1810 m, then contour below the steep section and head south

---

[ii] Editor's Note: Though you are technically in a newly-established BC Parks "core area", which doesn't allow random camping, you will not be hassled up there if you are through-travellers respecting the environment. BC Parks used a height of land boundary for the core area, so this location was included by default rather than by design. The core area was created to control camping and campfires in the heavily-used lower elevation area of the Forbidden Plateau.

towards main summit. You can either avoid the summit by turning west and descending a rockslide, then back up to the ridge, or go up and over the summit, which is not as hard as it looks [3].

Proceeding south from Mount George V, follow the height of land. At the 1600-m level drop off ridge to the right, as a cliff band ahead (not shown on the map) blocks the direct route to the col. A game trail, leading to a small slide area to the right of the ridge, is easy to follow [4]. Do not drop down the west side any more than necessary for easy contouring around the cliffs, then get back up to the col. The upper end of Siokum Creek valley is one of the few sheltered spots on the route, and has some good camping areas.

The main route south is joined by a route from Ralph River at the point marked [5], and continues on a height of land past Ink Lake and on to Aureole snowfield. (Note: Ralph Ridge is a viable escape route.) Follow a line of rock cairns, positioned where necessary to avoid steep sections. Hike south up the snowfield to a low point between the summits of Rees Ridge, then head roughly southeast down the main ridge towards the col between Milla Lake and Mirren Lake.

If you are going west to Flower Ridge by way of Tzela Lake you now have a choice of routes:

If you are hikers rather than climbers, and want to avoid any exposure and use of a rope handline for security, leave Rees Ridge at the 1780-m level and pick your way down the steep southwest side, then down a small side ridge to a point near the outlet of Milla Lake. Cross Shepherd Creek and contour around, a little below the 1230-m level, using open areas, then hike south up the glacier on the west side of Mount Harmston, keeping to the west side of the valley to stay clear of steep snow sections. This small glacier does not normally have any dangerous crevasses, but in the last few years of warm winters the ice has become more exposed. Keep to the right side near the top, over the pass and down to regain the main route at the snout of Cliffe Glacier. You have to drop 300 metres lower this way.

If you are climbers, you may choose to follow down the ridge in a southeast direction from [6]. There are good campsites on the south-facing slope of this ridge. From the col below Rees Ridge, the escarpment looks very spectacular but the route is quite easy, proving the truth of a well-known climber's advice: "you can't judge a mountain till you rub your nose on it" (the late Rex Gibson). On leaving the col, keep up the ridge to the small glacier, bearing right to follow the moraine between the snow and the top of cliffs above Moving Glacier (exposed). This brings you to a steep gully across your path which runs from the base of the cliffs above [7]. Cross this near its top, using a rope for steep and exposed sections, contour slightly up and across the slope to the right for about 90 metres, then climb straight up at the bottom of the cliff to a steep short gully which runs off to the right across the face. Follow this to its top, then climb up a short pitch and you are on the main ridge with Comox Glacier to your left and Argus Mountain and The Red Pillar to your right.

(b) Comox Glacier to Flower Ridge (Maps D4, C4 and C5)

Continuing from the point where you gained the main ridge, follow a game trail over the small summit at the head of Moving Glacier (steep snow early in the season) and down to the base of the northeast ridge of Argus Mountain. Leave the ridge at this point and angle down across the snow slope on southeast side of Argus to the base of south cliffs, and contour across the south-facing scree slopes above the lower cliffs, working down near the top of lower cliffs, then up again at about 1720 m. The first part of the route around the cliff will be steep, exposed snow before July, but it is usually possible to go between the snow and the rocks at the base of the cliff.

The route down off Argus onto Cliffe Glacier is easy if you pick the correct gully (which used to be marked by a rock cairn: will somebody please rebuild it?) and small chimney [8]. Where this gully opens out above a steep section, contour right, then down to the snow. Be cautious here, because where the glacier has melted back it leaves a hard sediment which looks like sand but provides little purchase. High speed, torn clothes and a skinned rear end are likely results. Wear your crampons.

Continue across the glacier southwest to a small low ridge paralleling the west side of the glacier. From here [9] you have a choice of two routes to Tzela Lake. The first starts down near the base of the steep part of The Red Pillar, and into a small side valley leading down to the meadows on the east side of the lake. This is the best route for going to the lake only. The second route goes down a small ridge alongside the glacier. Keep to the glacier side near the lower end and cross the creek below the snout; if the creek is very high you will have to wade across at the snout. Go into the timber facing the end of the ridge, find a game trail about 15 metres above the creek and, staying high, well above the creek [10], contour around till you reach an open area. Follow this around to the open flower slopes that angle down to the northwest, and to the large upper flower meadows on the main valley floor. From these meadows, southwards down to Tzela Lake, there is a good game trail which stays on the east side of the stream and leads to camping areas at the north end of the lake.

For the Shepherd Creek ridge route, continue northwards up the main valley to a pass [38]. See also Section 2, route (g), page 60.

The Flower Ridge route goes west, across the meadows at about the 1280-m level and, staying to the left of a small side creek and contouring around on open slopes [11], goes up the ridge to the 1540m level. This upper route will avoid the bushy sections encountered on the lower route starting at Tzela Lake. From here, follow the watershed ridge between the Ash River and Henshaw Creek.

Map C5

The unnamed peak at the head of Henshaw Creek can be bypassed by contouring at the 1600-m level around its southeast side to a small lake at the head of Henshaw Creek. Then follow the ridge centre right up to Flower Ridge.

(c) Flower Ridge to Cream Lake and Bedwell Lake (Map C5)

Continue southwards, dropping off Flower Ridge at the 1660-m level, into the narrow col [12] between Price Creek and Margaret Lake. From this col there are only two choices if you are hiking: **south**, around the east side of Mount Rosseau and Misthorn [iii] to Love Lake or, eventually, Cream Lake, or **west** to join the main trail to Cream Lake. Experienced mountaineers equipped for technical climbing may follow the ridge (not straightforward) south to the summit of Mount Rosseau, or travel directly to Cream Lake by traversing the north-facing slopes of Septimus and Rosseau. These two routes to Cream Lake are hazardous and are not shown on the maps. They are described below for the benefit of mountaineers only.

Safe route for hikers: Continue down Price Creek valley taking advantage of clear areas at lower end of slides as much as possible. Join Price Creek trail as soon as possible and follow it up to Cream Lake. This will be hard going in the bushy sections until the trail from Price Creek to Margaret Lake is finished, but it is the only safe route for hikers. It may not look very far from Flower Ridge to Cream Lake, but allow a day for it.

Alternate route for hikers: Follow the ridge south for a kilometre and contour around to the south side of Mount Rosseau staying below the remnants of glaciers and snow fields. From here hikers to Della Falls Trail can follow a good route to Love Lake (see page 25). Cross the ridge just below the summit of Mount Septimus and descend a snow slope to a good camping site at the south end of Cream Lake. There is also good camping at the outfall of the lake. This area is very fragile and showing the impact of its popularity. Your very best no-impact techniques should be stringently applied, including using a stove, not making a campfire, properly burying your excrement (or packing it out) and carefully flaming your toilet paper.

[iii] Misthorn is now (1994) the official name of the generic peak just east of Mount Rosseau. The name comes from A.O. Wheeler's journal when the Alpine Club of Canada climbed in Strathcona Park in 1912.

Upper climbing route: Goes across the top of the glacier above Green Lake, contouring around under a hanging glacier and down to Cream Lake. This route (not shown on our map) is for experienced climbers and only under the best of conditions. For the average hiker there are too many dangers from rock and ice fall.

Middle route for experienced climbers: Turn west at the north side of the col and descend to the small green lake on the moraine; follow along the north side of this and cross at the outlet (Price Creek), then contour around under the cliff, taking advantage of open areas and a game trail, until you come to a break in the mountain which forces you down and a little to the right. The rope is needed for a 12-metre cliff [13] before you reach an open area at the base of the first large slide coming off Mount Septimus. If you wish to avoid the cliff and don't mind slide alder, continue down alongside Price Creek, and come across to the open area as soon as possible, but don't get down too low. Continuing, climb straight up the big slide, working to the right and keeping out of alder till you get near the base of the cliffs where there is a good game trail; follow this along cliffs [14], keeping above the bush in slides; cross over creek coming down from the hanging glacier. Here you will have to go up again, contouring towards Cream Lake as much as possible. The route is not hard to find as there is only one feasible way (glacier above and slides below) and it will put you on the gentle slope above the east side of Cream Lake, with an easy hike down to good campsites at the outlet.

Continuing on to Bedwell Lake, follow game trail around north side of Cream Lake, turn right when you come to the view of Della Falls and go west up the small side ridge to the 1350-m level, then follow a bench that continues along this contour (good area for flowers) to the Drinkwater/Bedwell pass. Beyond the pass, on the Bedwell side, go around the north side of the little lake near the watershed. Continue down an open draw to about the 1140-m level, then contour along the side of the ridge and work into the centre as you near the bottom. There is a good game trail with old tapes [15], which is easy to follow and avoids small drops at the centre of the ridge.

51

At the bottom of the ridge area by Bedwell Lake there is a BC Parks campsite with pit toilets. (Cream Lake to Bedwell Lake: allow 3 hours). Note: no campfires allowed.

(d) Bedwell Lake to Burman Lake (Maps C5, B5, B4 and B3)

Allow 5 days. This section of the route is characterized by glaciated granite, with many hidden drops which must be circumnavigated. From the camping area, go north [iv] on the main trail and gain the route around Bedwell Lake by crossing the outfall of Baby Bedwell Lake. Stay close to the lake shore, and after crossing a stream at the most westerly point of the lake turn west and ascend a moderate slope to about the 1100-m level. From here, the route to the summit of Mount Tom Taylor continues southwest up a prominent ridge, and the cross country route to Burman Lake turns north, crossing a creek [17] just below its lake outlet and bluff. Ascend the small side ridge north of this lake and head up to the Bedwell/Moyeha pass, then travel northwest following the centre of a ridge for about 800 m.

Map B5

A steep section leads down about 220 metres [18] to a very attractive camping area looking across to Taylor Glacier. Continue north by way of a flat open ridge to the lake on the Moyeha River drainage south of Thelwood Lake, bear left at steep section near the bottom and cross the creek a short way below the outlet. This is the lowest elevation (850 m) on the entire tour. Here, in the western section of the park, north-facing slopes and level areas are open heather due to heavy winter snowfall. South-facing slopes can be bushy (rhododendron) to the 1080-m level.

From the valley floor hike west up centre of ridge lying south of Greenview Lake, which is bushy and a little hard to get onto at the lower level, but well-defined and clear going above 950 m. The hump south of Greenview Lake can be contoured around on its southwest side at the 1080-m level, then up into a beautiful, hanging valley with arrowhead-shaped lakes and good camping areas.

[iv] Earlier editions of this book showed routes through the area south of Bedwell Lake. Because there are numerous bears in this area, BC Parks is requesting that hikers stay out of that area, and our route descriptions have been modified accordingly.

Map B4

Continue west past the lakes and swing up to the saddle on the east ridge of Moyeha Mountain, and down the other side in a north-westerly direction to about the 1100-m level. At this point [19], you have a choice: around Mount Thelwood or over it.

For the route around, drop down and cross the creek (open going) then head north up the gully and open slope west of main creek leading to the little square lake east of Mount Thelwood. This section makes for very difficult going when there is no snowpack. The east side of the creek does not offer a better alternative. (For a side trip, well worth the effort, go down to the Upper Thelwood Lake and flower meadows.) Pass the "square" lake [20] and go on through the meadows, dropping down to about 1230m, then contour around on game trail under the cliffs (don't drop too low) to reach heather meadows north of Mount Thelwood.

For the route over Mount Thelwood, contour left from [19] into the pass at base of southwest ridge, then straight up this ridge to the summit, then north across snowfield and so on down to the heather meadows. It is a good route if you have the energy and weather is clear.

From here go north and a little to the east, crossing the low point of an alpine ridge northeast of Thelwood, that divides the north and south branches of Myra Creek [21]. This narrow and well-defined ridge continues eastwards down to the fork. Below 1080 m the ridge is very bushy, but a route has been flagged from here down to the Westmin mine site. See route (c), page 30.

Continuing the main route from [21], drop down 30 metres or so, then contour left at about the 1140-m level, up to left of a round hump and a little lake, then north to open slopes leading to the west. Contour around at this level and up to the ridge near the lakes to join the alternate route.

An alternate route to this point, from the heather meadows north of Mount Thelwood, involves more climbing and takes you higher than the above.

Hike west [22] from these meadows, and through a pass to an attractive meadows at the head of Bancroft Creek. From the northeast side of this meadow turn north and go up, past a steep area on the right, then east to the 1600-m level. Descend the north ridge and swing right after passing lakes below you on the east side, then generally northwards down a steep section to the outlet of a lake which is part of the Burman River watershed.

Continue north into the timber and contour to the right at 1020 m, then up to the head of a large lake from which issues the north fork of Myra Creek (bushy at low levels). A less bushy route goes east, up the centre of a ridge [23] to a point opposite the west end of the large lake, then down to a heather meadow. This involves about 300 metres of climbing, but is well worth it if the bushes are wet. Head north around west end of the lake and climb a 30-m steep section, staying a little to the right. When open alpine is reached, continue north up a gradual slope and past a small lake near the ridge centre, then east along the centre of the ridge to the west peak of Phillips Ridge. Bear right at the steep parts of the lower levels [24]. Halfway up the ridge, the route leaves area of glaciated granite. East of this peak turn north and descend a limestone ridge.

Map B3

After 1½ km, **an alternate route** to Schjelderup Lake drops to the west, avoiding the routefinding difficulties and steep terrain of the main route, as follows. From the lowest point on Phillips Ridge descend the gully to the west for about 80 m and then traverse to the right at a low angle towards the outlet of the lake. It is a bit scrubby and there is the odd small bluff. There is no trail. Cross the stream and contour around the south side of the lake in open terrain. There is good camping at the end of the lake. Follow the stream up to another small lake under Mount Burman and then traverse a small ridge to Schjelderup Lake. Contour around the lake on the west side staying about 40-50 m above the lake for the easiest line. You are now on the normal route, having avoided a significant elevation gain along Phillips Ridge and, more importantly, some very difficult route-finding between the north end of the ridge and the lake.

The traditional route follows Phillips Ridge northwards to a col east of Schjelderup Lake [25]. The Marble Meadows route continues north.

Schjelderup Lake (looking southeast).

For the Golden Hinde area find a game trail leading steeply down through the meadows and follow it to the end of the meadows and through a thick grove of trees to a very steep grassy clearing with a stream on the right (north). Cross the stream. The route contours to the northwest under the last set of cliffs (at about 1420m) to gain a side ridge coming up from the lake outlet. The trick is to go below the cliffs, otherwise you bluff out later, but not drop down too far and miss the easy going through mature timber on the relatively obscure ridge. Follow down this, just north of centre. As with most east-west ridges between 1080 m and 1540 m in this area, there is clear going a few feet north of ridge centre, due to heavy snow pack. The other side is often bushy.

From a campsite at the lake outlet [26] go up the northeast ridge of Mount Burman (clear going on northwest side), contour to the west under a steep section to a good ledge leading up and across to join the north ridge below cliffs at 1540 m. Follow this ridge down for about 100 m, then turn west down to meadows above the south bay of Burman Lake. An easy way down may be hard to find, as this is in a zone of glaciated granite. If backpacking to the Golden Hinde, continue north down the ridge (if you are bushbashing, and dangling down steep bits holding on to saplings like a trout on a hook, you are probably on the route) to the east end of Burman Lake, and up the open ridge to the base of the Hinde, camping near a small lake on the south side of the mountain if you intend to climb it. The Golden Hinde is usually climbed by its southeast ridge, attainable from this route by following to the east the northernmost gulley above the snowfield on the south side of the Hinde (directly above the small lake).

Contour northwest past the small lake directly southwest of The Behinde and follow the east side of the outflow stream [45]. This is a very tricky spot. The route of choice is a little exposed, and goes down, left, over the rocks before you reach the next stream. Two-thirds of the way down cut left into a shallow but reassuring crack which returns you to the outflow stream. A long handline can be very useful here. Descend the huge snow (boulder) bowl to rejoin the direct route from Burman Lake, which we now describe.

From the meadow above the south bay of Burman Lake, contour west at the 1230-m level and follow the northwest ridge of Mount Burman to the outlet of Burman Lake. This is not as even as it appears on the map, due to granite bluffs. Alternately, work down to the southwest bay [27] and follow the shoreline to the outlet.

(e) Burman Lake to Elk River Pass (Maps B3 and A2).

Allow three days. From the west end of Burman Lake hike north, up through open areas to about the 1230-m level. Drop down a little, turn west and, at the 1200-m level, contour below the rock bluffs. Game trails and old tapes make the route fairly easy to follow where gullies must be crossed. At the heather meadows west of the Hinde, turn north at the first small lake, keeping to an open area below some rock slides [28]. A fairly level route at the 1200-m level leads to a big rock slide coming off the west (Behinde) peak.

Cross at the base of this slide and up to a saddle between Burman and Wolf River watersheds. Hike west across this and up the southeast ridge of an unnamed mountain at the head of the Ucona River. Keep to the centre of this ridge, but go to the right at one steep spot at the 1350-m level. Near the south summit, turn north. Traverse the many small summits and descend a connecting ridge to Mount De Voe. At the lowest point go northwest, to contour around the meadows above some small lakes at 1260 m (where you can make a good camp), then north (following a creek not shown on NTS maps) up to a small col on the west ridge of Mount De Voe. Turn sharply west up a steep heather slope to about the 1600-m level, then turn north and follow the ridge centre.

Map A2

When you are overlooking a large round lake at the head of the west fork of Wolf River, hike northwest down a side ridge to the southwest corner of this lake [29]. (Good camping area.)

The route then follows the west side of this lake across an overgrown slide area at the base of a prominent cliff, and up through a strip of timber on the south side of a small creek. Staying in the creek bed itself is a preferred option. At the top, a good game trail continues along the south side of a small lake, then northwest across flower meadows and up a final 220 m to Elk River Pass.

This ascent is steep and no clear way is obvious. Angle up with the cliffs in sight on your right in order to gain the meadows. Descending the pass, be cautious of crossing old spring snow which has been undercut by the river.

For those going south from the Elk River Pass, a special note. Your best route drops steeply down the heather before angling left, and through mature forest, towards the Golden Hinde which you can now see in the far distance. You should stay well above and to the left of a prominent rock cliff you can see directly below. It's easier if you cross creeks and stay in the forest, than getting into a creek gulley and following it down. This section is difficult, and in many trips I haven't ever been the same way twice. **Editor.**

After the upper canyon the route follows the east side of the river, sometimes high up the side. Tape markers can usually be seen. Enter the forest at the 1020-m level and follow a game trail on the east side of the river, just under the cliffs [30], in order to avoid the lower canyon. When the valley turns northwest, continue down across rock slides and an open area, cross the river at the 880-m level, and take an elk trail down through the forest to the junction of the stream from Landslide Lake. This is where the main valley trail begins, and it follows the west bank of the Elk River. See page 36.

(f) Phillips Watershed High Ridge Tour (Maps C3, B3, B4, C4)

(For access by Phillips Ridge trail from Westmin mine site see Map C4 and description on page 29.)

Map C3

This is perhaps the most rewarding of the shorter high ridge routes, enabling the hiker with only a week to see the heart of the park. From Phillips Creek marine campsite (boat required for crossing Buttle Lake), follow the Marble Meadows trail to good camping at 1540-m level (5-7 hours). From here the direct route to the southwest ridge of Marble Peak bears a little right from the cairn, through a limestone section, and no height is lost. Cross the upper meadows by a good game trail to a col west of Marble Peak. By following this route, hiking traffic is directed away from the flower meadows around the lakes, already showing damage from over-use.

From this col there is a choice of routes to the area of the Wheaton Hut. (To climb Mount McBride from here allow 12 hours return).

Continue down, past the hut, up the next slope a short way and contour west at about the 1540-m level, above Wheaton Lake at the head of the north fork of Phillips Creek. A wide fault leads west to a 1600-m elevation ridge. You are aiming for [31] the prominent rock spire (Morrison Spire) which dominates your immediate western skyline.

Map B3

Follow the ridge centre to a col below a waterfall coming off the main north-south ridge from McBride; (the last bump may be contoured at the 1540-m level). Go up to 1620 m, then turn south along an exposed limestone fault (with fossils) and follow this line into the col north of Limestone Cap, where there is a good campsite if you need one. From here, or even earlier, it is worth your while to hike to the summit of Morrison Spire, which is easy from the back (southwest) side. Depending on the time of day you might have your lunch on top. Limestone Cap is a flat-topped rock escarpment, deeply fissured through rainwater erosion - a fascinating place to explore. Its south slope is deep with wildflowers in spring (usually July here).

The route from here follows the divide south and is straightforward to a small, flat, east-west ridge [32], just north of a 1820-m bump. This ridge has a cliff on its south side, not shown on the NTS map, which can be avoided by contouring into the col, following an exposed ledge and gully around the west side. There are three ledges, but the one you need goes right down to the col, with a short drop at the end, where packs must be handed down (easy to find going south to north). Continue south to the 1820-m summit (which can be avoided by traversing its east side, low down) and descend, keeping to the clear ground east of the ridge's centre [33], to a large col north of Greig Ridge (pronounced "Gregg"). Go up from this col to a good campsite at the west end of Greig Ridge, and take an easy side trip east along Greig Ridge to see the alpine flowers. The main route around the watershed continues southwest, left around a steep section near the summit and on down to a col [25] to meet with the Bedwell-Burman route.

Map B4

Continue south to the west peak of Phillips Ridge (where the Bedwell route turns west), and head southeast then follow the ridge east around the south side of the Phillips Creek watershed.

Map C4

The trail down to Westmin mine site leaves the plateau at Arnica Lake (see page 29). Continuing east on the circuit, avoid cliffs by keeping to a ridge between creeks to gain the main south ridge of Mount Phillips.

Map C3

Hike over Mount Phillips and along the narrow north ridge. Go over the north summit (1684 m) and keep to the north ridge. At a point where the ridge becomes broken, follow a good game trail at the top of the meadows on the east side. Continue north, leaving this game trail when it veers east. At the 1230-m level take the right-hand ridge leading down to Buttle Lake at Phillips Creek. If you started your circuit from the mine site, you must now continue up the Marble Meadows Trail; see also route (h), page 32.

(g) Routes around Ralph River, Shepherd Creek and Henshaw Creek Watersheds (Maps C3, D3, D4 and C4)

These need not be described in detail as the approaches to the main ridge route already described are quite straightforward, except for the following points:

Delight Lake ridge route leaves the road at the north end of Ralph River bridge. Cross a log jam at the junction of Shepherd Creek and Ralph River. The next section is bushy through a burn; keep within the sound of Shepherd Creek until you reach unburned timber, then angle back to the left, staying in old growth as much as possible until past the burn. Near the timberline, bear right to avoid cliffs.

Map D3

This is a good alternate way to Comox Glacier, leading up to the main route above Ink Lake. Contour across the triangular glacier north of Ink Lake and up its east side to gain the main ridge [5].

Map C3

The route up the ridge between Shepherd and Henshaw Creeks leaves the road at the creek which enters above a small bay 2.8 km south of Ralph River campground.

Map C4

Start up on the right side of the creek following a game trail, alongside a rock bluff, to a more open area under some mature forest. Staying on the south side of the creek, continue southeast up to the centre of the ridge. It is clear going under old growth to the alpine zone, but keep clear of an old burn near Shepherd Creek.

Map D4

The summit ridge involves some climbing, but this can be avoided (given safe conditions) by contouring across the snow slope to the glacier. An alternative route credited to Albert Hestler avoids snow slopes but adds some steep hiking. It leaves the main route at [37] to drop down to the lake, regaining the main route at [38]. After the summit, contour across glaciers to pass north of Tzela Lake.

(h) Augerpoint Route to Mount Albert Edward (Maps C3, D2)

A difficult route, only suitable for experienced hikers. The route has been marked right across with cairns, but the area is subject to considerable changes from year to year and cairns are often covered with snow well into the summer. From the foot of the ridge, at the Buttle Lake roadside, to the first good campsite takes about 2 hours, and 5 hours to the upper lakes. See also (b), page 31.

Map D2

From Ruth Masters Lake there are cairns and the odd splash of paint on the rocks till you come to the foot of the south ridge leading to Mount Albert Edward. There is only one place to get up, staying as far to the right as possible (but it is not signed or cairned). Conversely, if going from Mount Albert Edward, turn west on the long ridge and go down off it, but there is only one place to go down (not signed). Note: there is a 2,800 ft elevation advantage if you hike this route westwards from Paradise Meadows.

(i) Thelwood area from Mount Myra (Maps C4 and B4)

From Tennent Lake dam follow the route around the north side of the lake and continue west. However, from the top of Mount Myra the route is as follows: from the trail above the small alpine lake, follow the height of land west as shown on the map. All this route is over glaciated granite and is not as easy as the map would indicate, but it is completely free of bush.

(j) Drinkwater Creek to Price Creek (Map C5)

From the north end of Della Falls trail, the route to the head of the Drinkwater Creek valley goes through a slide area. Pick your way up, taking advantage of gravel bars where possible. Travel is mostly up the creek bed itself, especially the last half-kilometre up to the waterfall. It is not possible to avoid the water, so be prepared for wet feet. Where the valley turns northwest, keep to the right of a waterfall and then follow the valley's centre to Drinkwater Pass, usually on snow. Here you join the main route described between Cream Lake and Bedwell Lake, and the route from Price Creek described in (c) this section, page 50.

(k) Elk River Trail south to Elk River Pass (Maps A1 and A2).

From the gravel flats a kilometre below Landslide Lake, cross a new bridge to the east side of the creek coming down from Landslide Lake. The elk trail enters the forest about 100 m up the west bank of the Elk River. Following the valley southeastwards, this clearly-defined trail eventually crosses to the northeast side of the river, which is open going to a stand of trees where there is excellent camping. Beyond this, find your way through thick slide alder growing over a rock slide from Elkhorn. Here the elk trail climbs to the base of the cliffs and continues up the valley at this level, crossing side gullies. When clear of the canyon, angle down to the stream. Here the timber ends and the valley floor is open. Generally follow the west side of the creek leading to the pass.

(l) Elkhorn Mountain access route (Map A1)

Follow the Elk River Trail for $2\frac{1}{2}$ km and cross the river to where the route begins on the south side of a prominent creek. This route is now fairly obvious and frequently flagged. Stay to the right at steep sections. Most groups with full packs will take 6-7 hours to reach the usual camp site (see map A1). From here it is 4-5 hours to the summit. Camping here leaves enough time to hike out to your car that same day. The route to the summit is not for hikers who are not also rockclimbers. There is lots of exposure, loose rock, possible rappels and intricate route finding - serious stuff. Caution is required, and the assurance of a climbing rope.

KEY TO STRATHCONA PARK MAPS

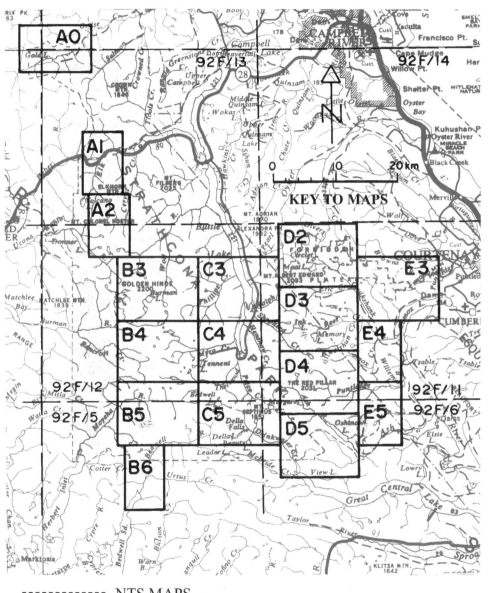

KEY TO MAPS

------------ NTS MAPS
———————— MAPS IN THIS BOOK

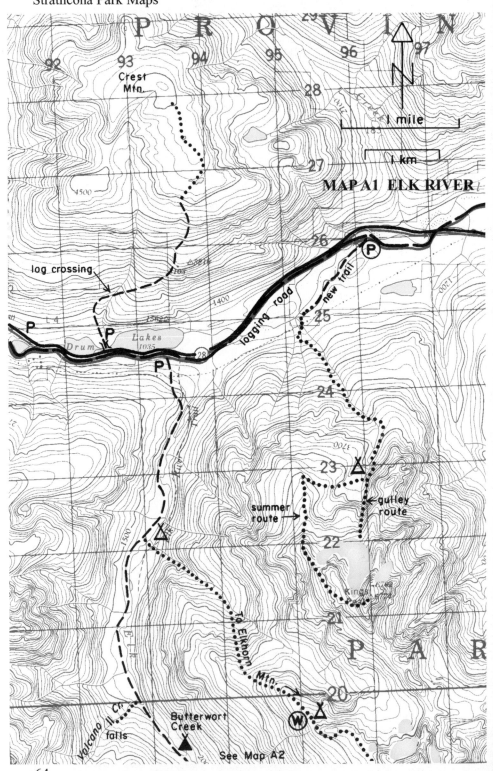

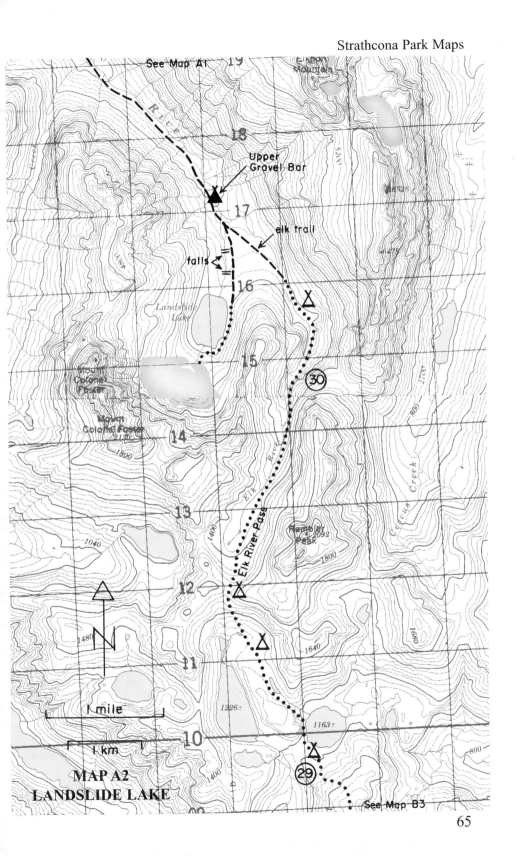

MAP A2
LANDSLIDE LAKE

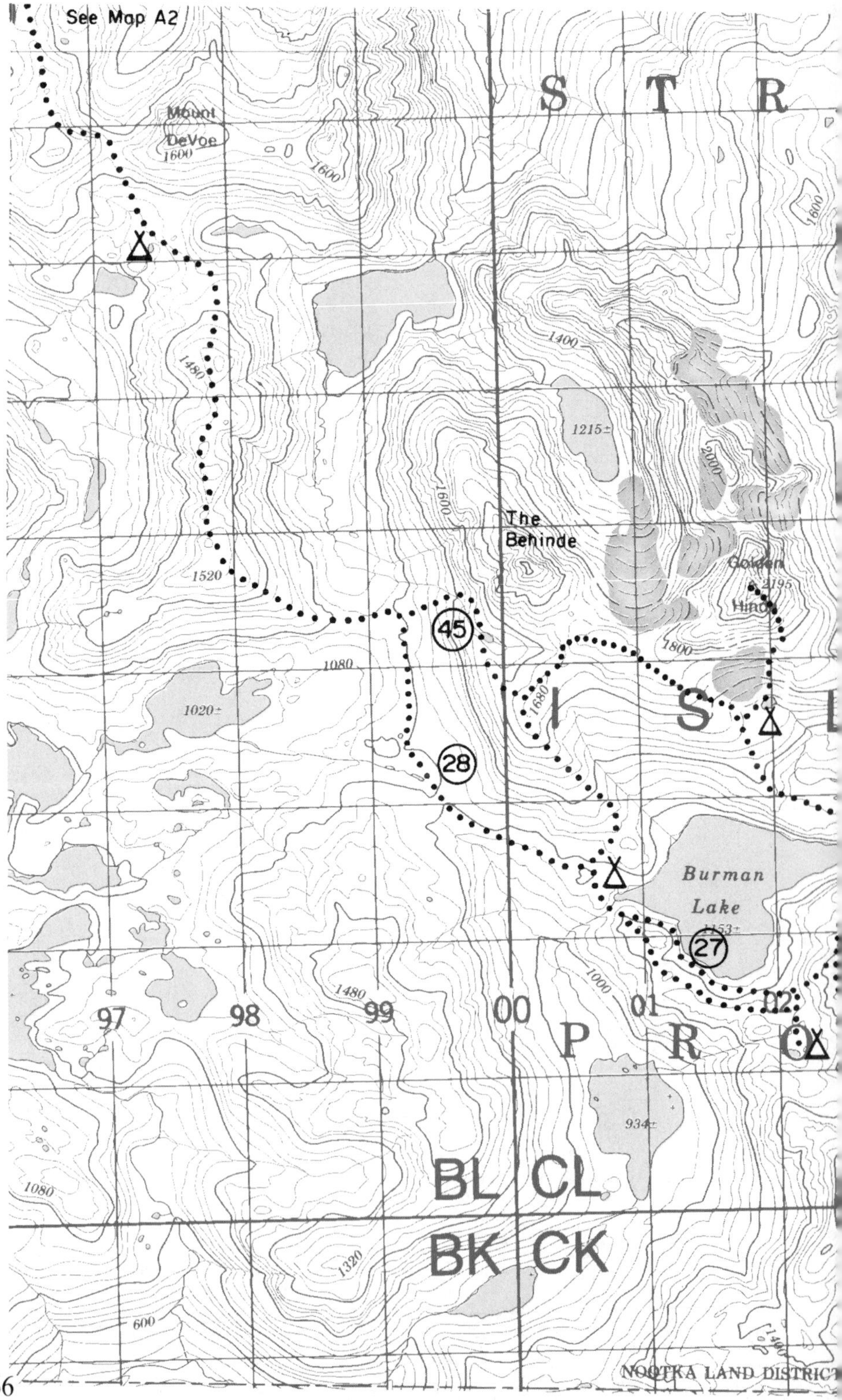

See Map A2

S T R

Mount
DeVoe
1600

1600

1600

1600

1400

1215±

2000

1600

The
Behinde

Golden
2195
Hind

45

1520

1080

I

1680

S

L

1020±

28

Burman
Lake
1153±

27

97

98

1480 99

1000

00

01

P

R

02

934±

BL CL

BK CK

1080

1320

600

NOOTKA LAND DISTRICT

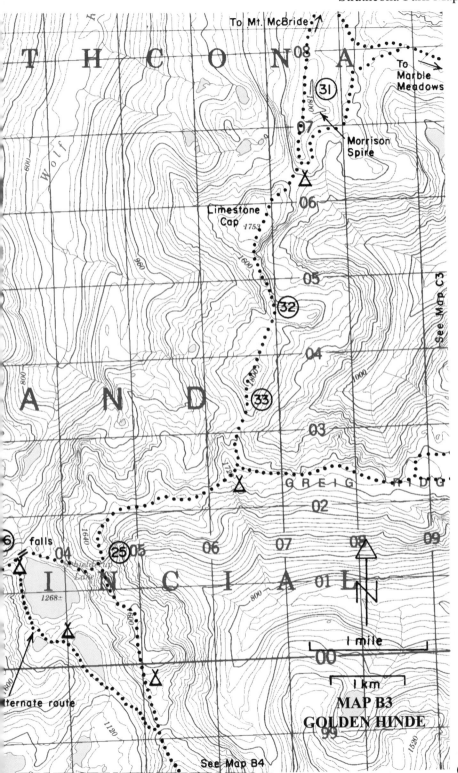

To Mt. McBride

To Marble Meadows

THCONA

31

Morrison Spire

Limestone Cap 1753

32

33

AND

GREIG RIDGE

falls

25

INCIA L

1268±

alternate route

1 mile

1 km

MAP B3
GOLDEN HINDE

See Map B4

See Map C3

Wolf

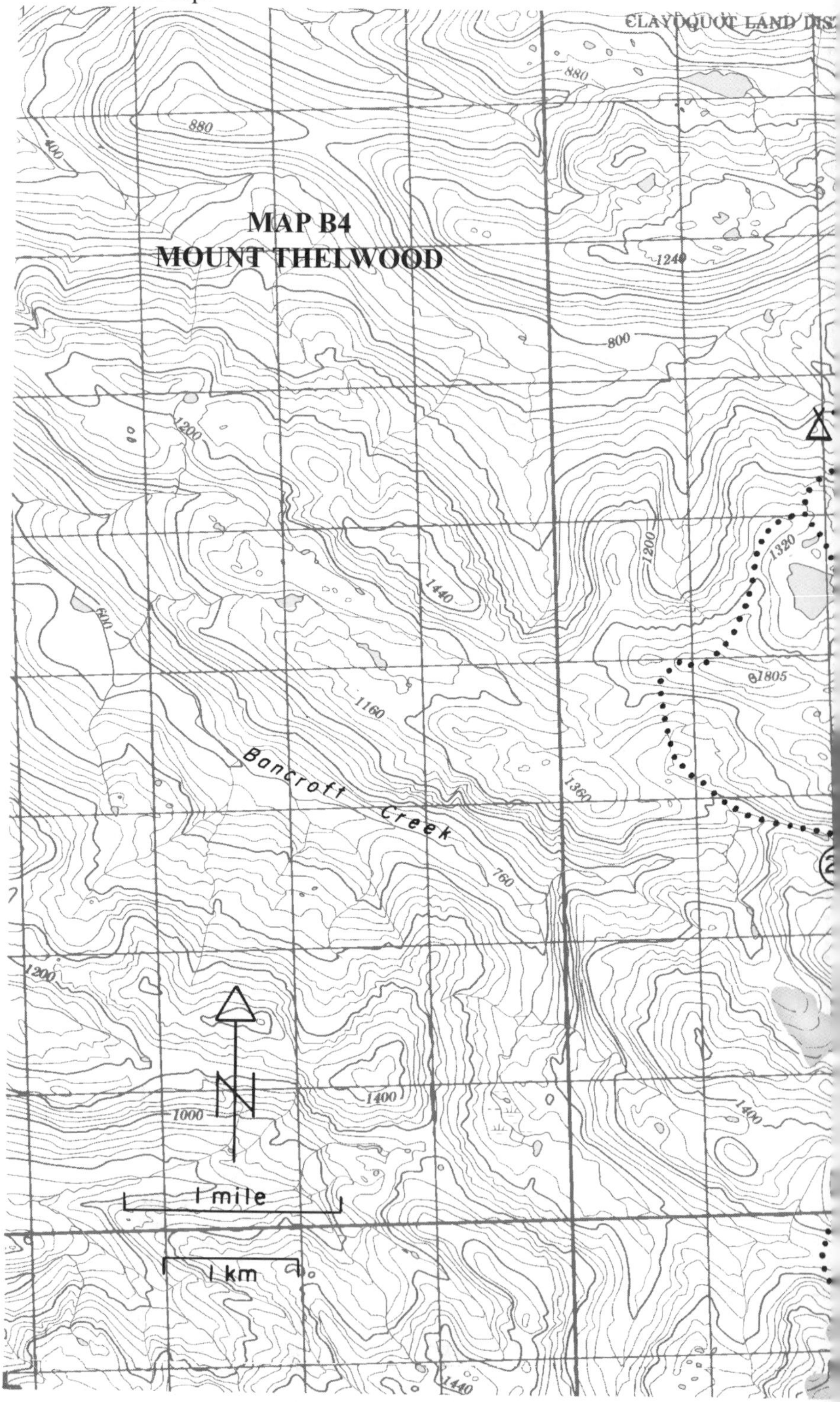

MAP B4
MOUNT THELWOOD

See Map B3

98

24

Phillips · 1732± 97 Ridge

Park Boundary

1320

1400

1600

1075±

S

less bushy

1360

96

1200

95

A

800 Myra

1120

A R K 94 Upper Myra Falls

1040 600

93

See Map C4

21

92 1160

840

1400 McNish Lake

91

Carwithen Creek

20 1440

1560 Carwithen Lake

90

1200 1400

Upper Thelwood Lake 1008±

89

19 Thelwood 1360

Carwithen Creek

See Map B5 Creek 972

Greenview Lake

88

87

86

River

85

Taylor G

Iceft

P R O V

See Map C5

84

83

82

81

80

ford crossing

(42) RIVE

PARK

EDWELL

rapids

Twin Falls Canyon

79

Ash

71

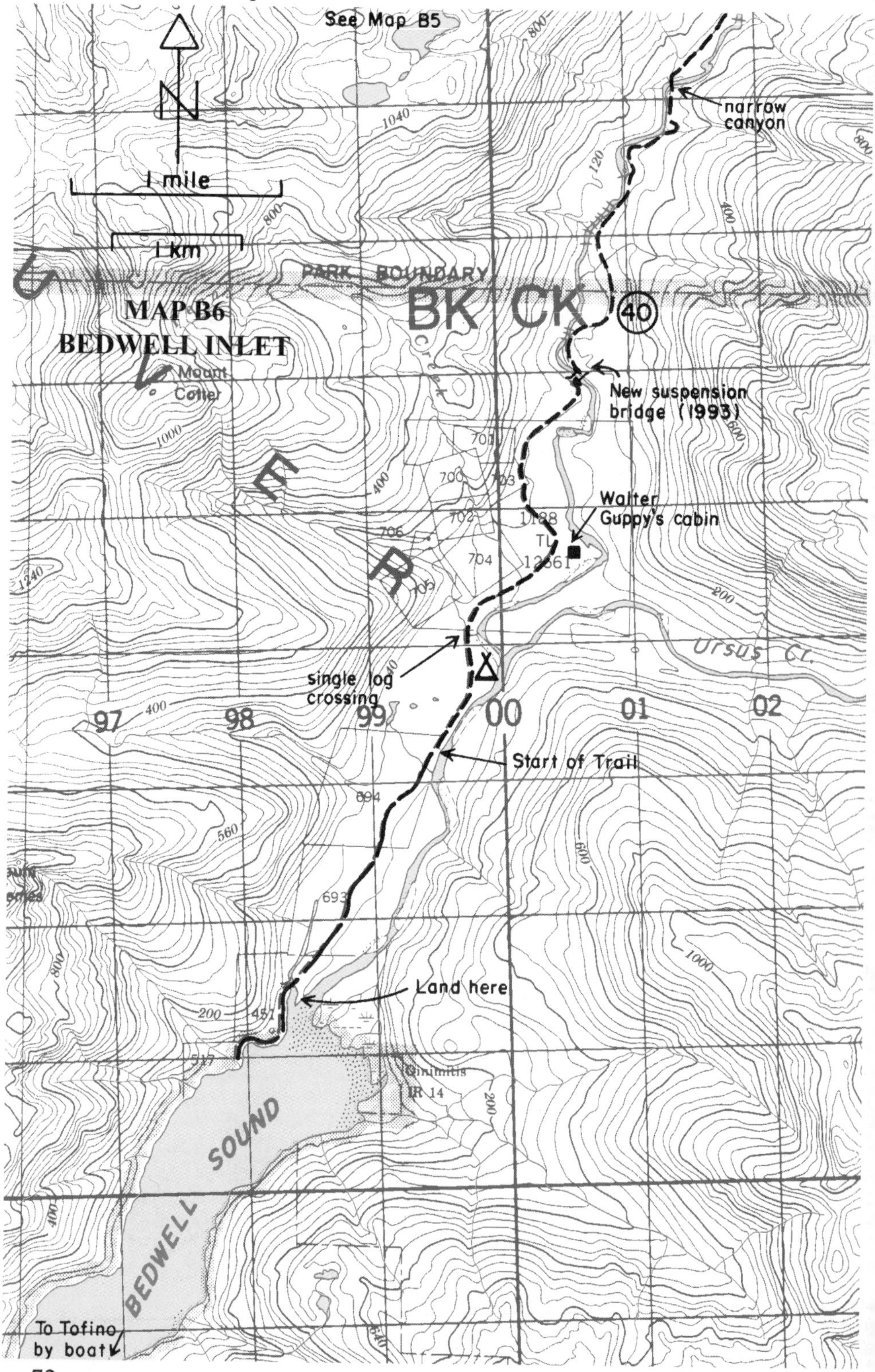

See Map B5

narrow
canyon

N

1 mile

1 km

PARK BOUNDARY

MAP B6
BEDWELL INLET

BK CK 40

Mount
Colter

New suspension
bridge (1993)

701

700 703

702 1438
704 T!
705 12361

706

Walter
Guppy's cabin

Ursus Cr.

single log
crossing

97 98 99 00 01 02

Start of Trail

894

560

693

1000

Land here 457

Qinimitis
IR 14

BEDWELL SOUND

To Tofino
by boat

Aerial view northwards from Della Lake (foreground),
to Love Lake, Cream Lake and Buttle Lake

1640

hut

Marblerock
Lake

Marble
Peak
1767

Wheaton
Lake

1600

Globe
Flower
Lake

MARBLE MEADOWS

1560

Marsh
Marigold
Lake

Limestone
Lake

MARBLE MEADOWS
TRAIL

W

See Map B3

1200

Phillips

Creek

(North)

400

R   A   N   G   E

Greig
Lake

Creek

1200

Greig Creek

800

1600

10   11   12   13   14   15

800

400

Phillips

600

game
trail

1400

Mount
Phillips

1600

1200

Park Boundary

See Map C4

74

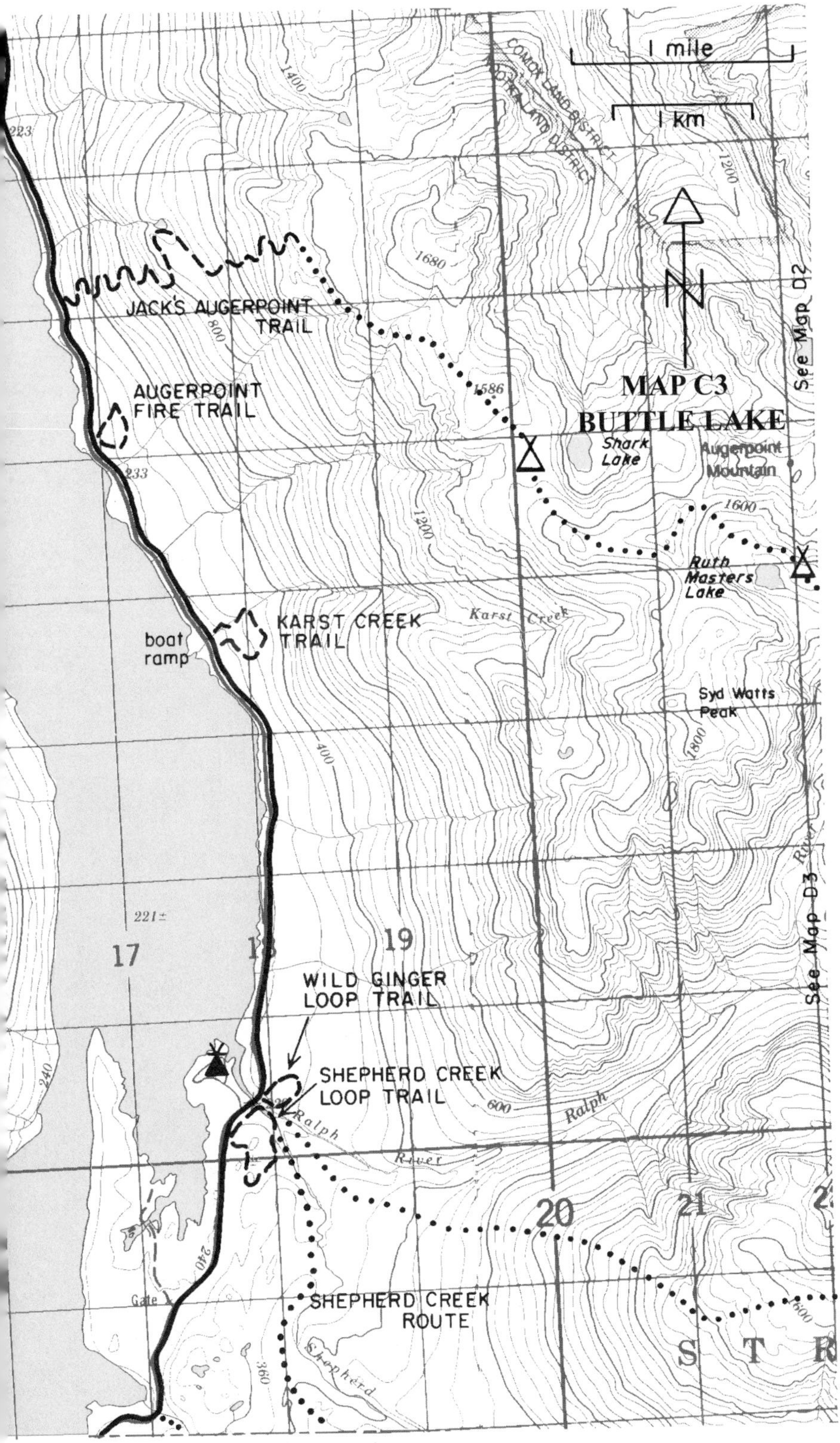
1 mile
1 km
COMOX LAND DISTRICT
NOOTKA LAND DISTRICT
MAP C3
BUTTLE LAKE
See Map D2
See Map D3
JACK'S AUGERPOINT
TRAIL
AUGERPOINT
FIRE TRAIL
Shark
Lake
Augerpoint
Mountain
Ruth
Masters
Lake
KARST CREEK
TRAIL
boat
ramp
Karst Creek
Syd Watts
Peak
WILD GINGER
LOOP TRAIL
SHEPHERD CREEK
LOOP TRAIL
Ralph
River
SHEPHERD CREEK
ROUTE
Shepherd
Gate
17
18
19
20
21
S T R
1400
1680
1586
1200
1600
1800
800
400
600
360
240
223
233
221±

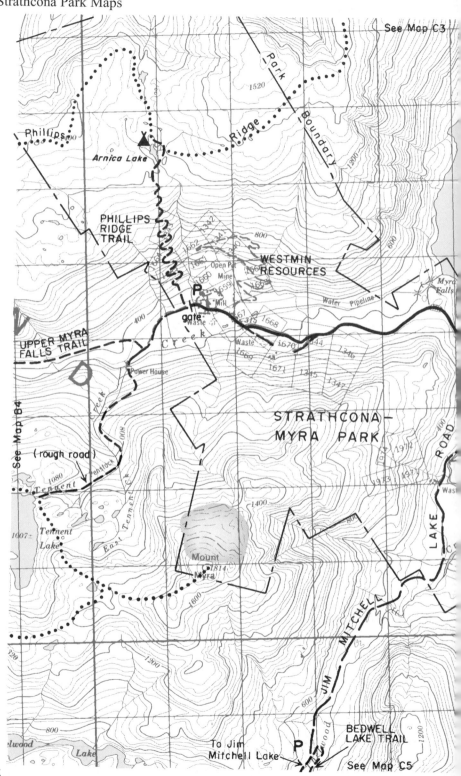

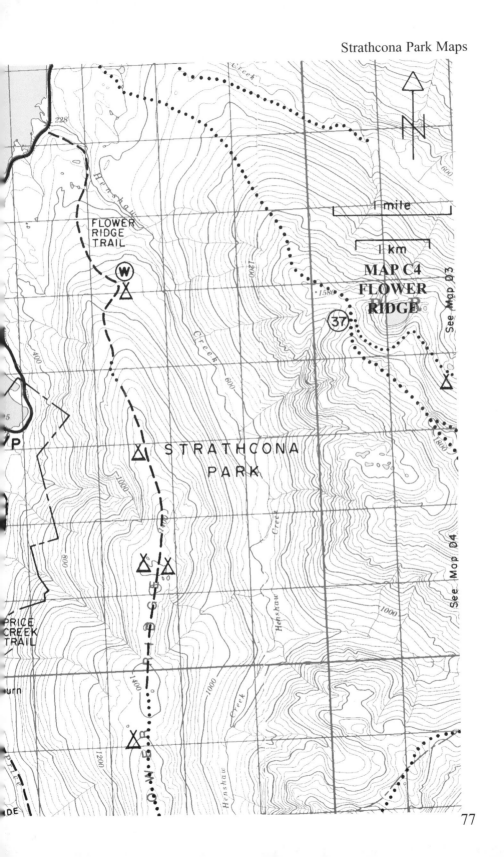

FLOWER
RIDGE
TRAIL

MAP C4
FLOWER
RIDGE

S T R A T H C O N A
P A R K

PRICE
CREEK
TRAIL

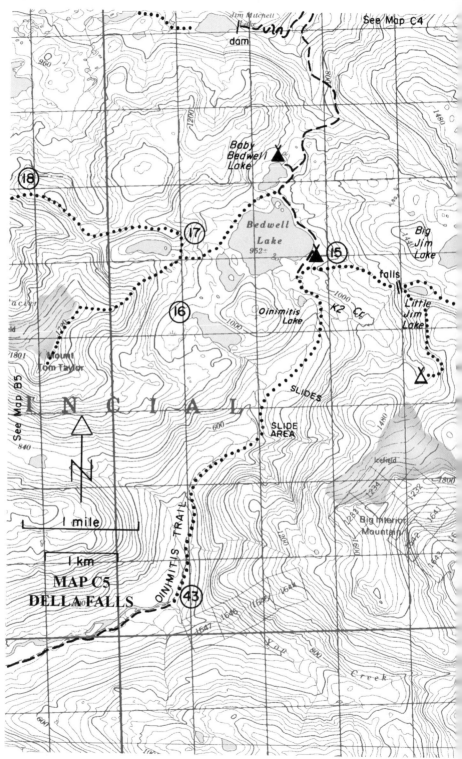

MAP C5
DELLA FALLS

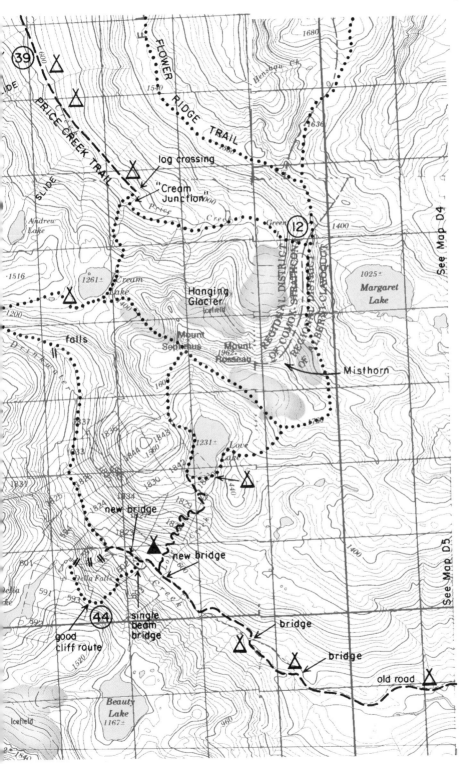

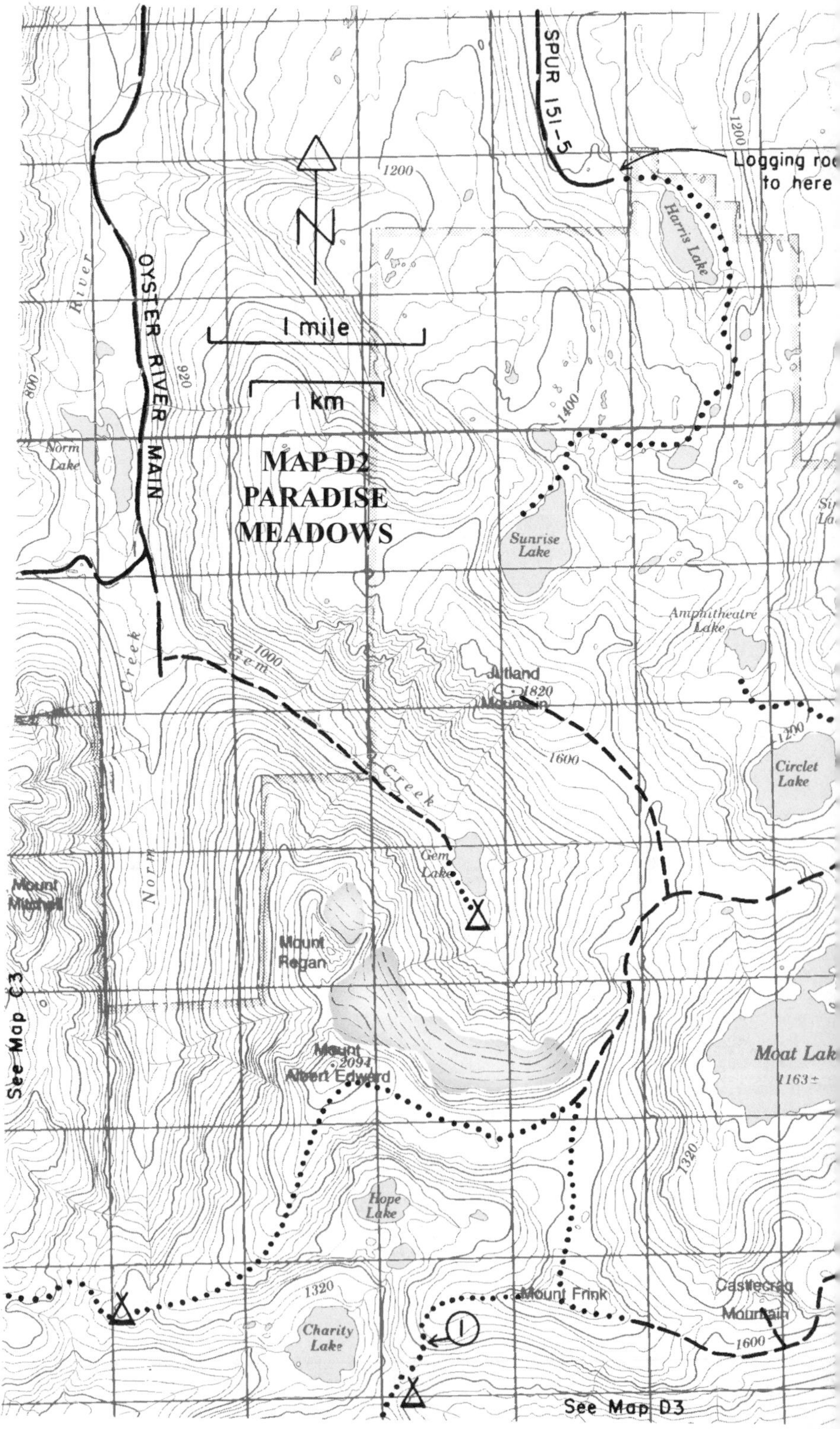

MAP D2
PARADISE
MEADOWS

1 mile

1 km

SPUR 151-5

Logging road
to here

Harris Lake

OYSTER RIVER MAIN

River

Norm Lake

Sunrise Lake

Amphitheatre Lake

Sir Lake

Gem Creek

Jutland Mountain
·1820

1600

Circlet Lake

1200

Gem Lake

Mount Mitchell

Mount Regan

Mount Albert Edward
2094

Moat Lake
1163±

Norm Creek

See Map C3

Hope Lake

1320

Mount Frink

Castlecrag Mountain

1600

Charity Lake

See Map D3

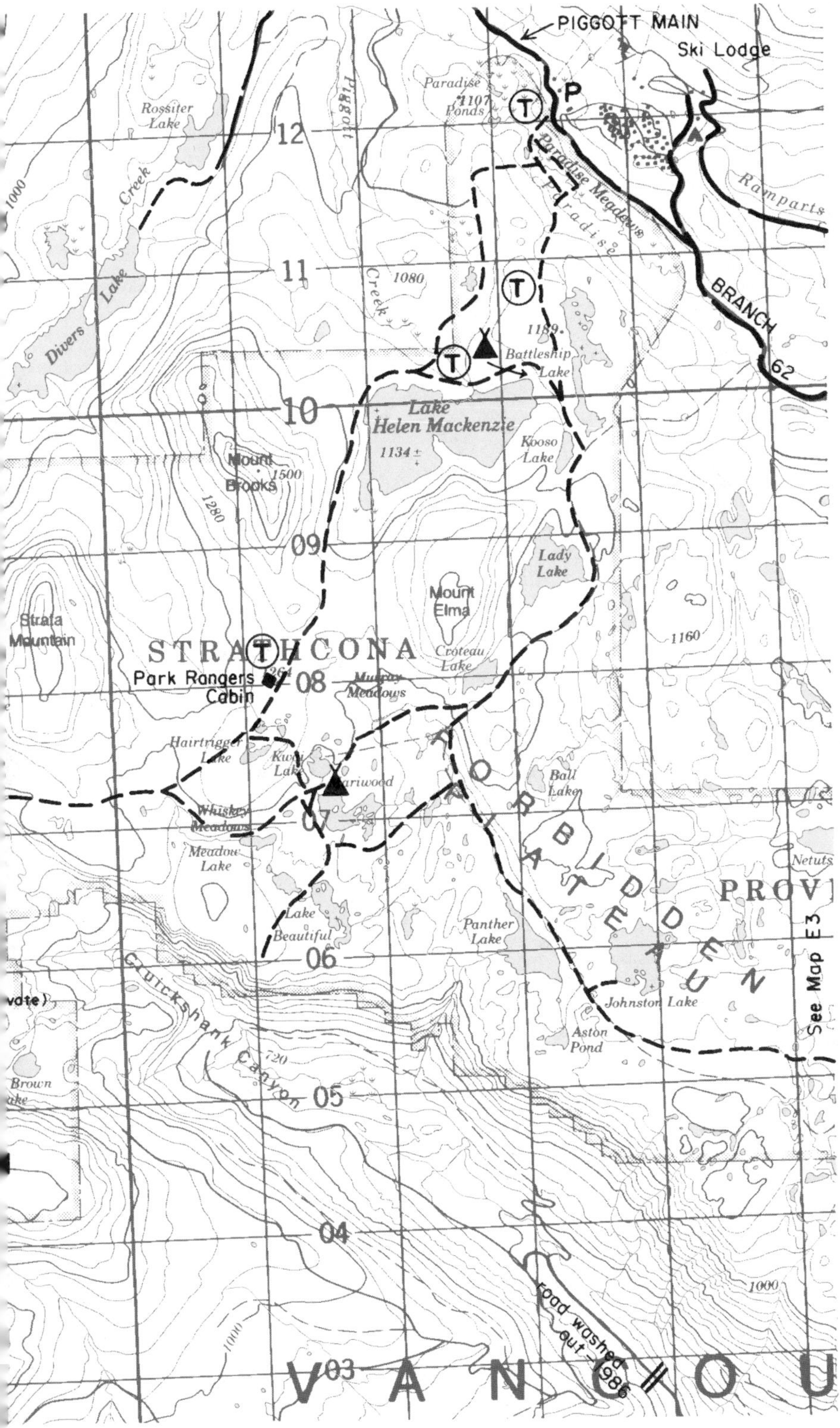
PIGGOTT MAIN
Ski Lodge
Paradise Ponds
Paradise Meadows
Ramparts
BRANCH 62
Rossiter Lake
Piggott Creek
Divers Lake
Battleship Lake
Lake Helen Mackenzie
Kooso Lake
Mount Brooks
Lady Lake
Mount Elma
Strata Mountain
STRATHCONA
Park Rangers Cabin
Croteau Lake
Murray Meadows
Hairtrigger Lake
Kwai Lake
Ball Lake
Whiskey Meadows
Meadow Lake
Lake Beautiful
Panther Lake
FORBIDDEN PLATEAU
PROV
Netuts
See Map E3
Johnston Lake
Aston Pond
Cruickshank Canyon
Brown Lake
Road washed out 1986
VANCOU

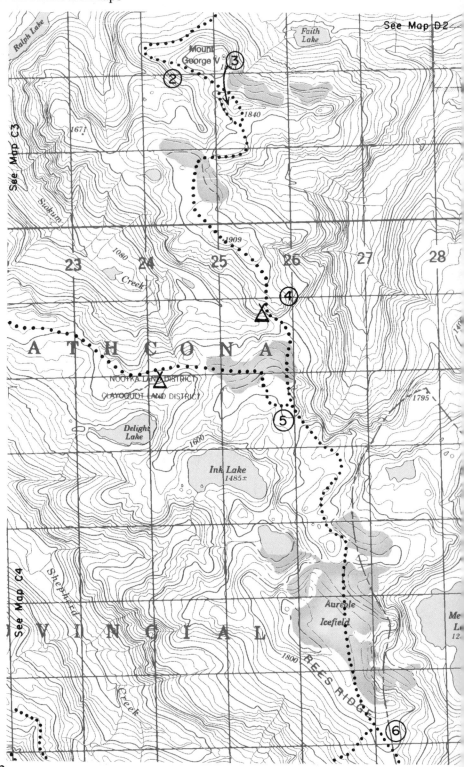

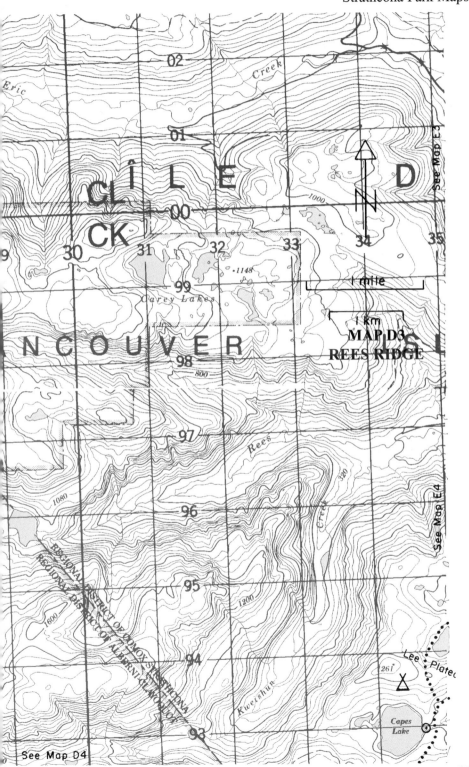

CLICK

CÎLED D

NCOUVER ISL

N

Eric

Creek

02

01

00

30   31   32   33   34   35

9

1000

1 mile

1 km

MAP D3
REES RIDGE

•1148

Carey Lakes

99

98

800

97

Rees

96

1080

95

1200

1600

94

261

Kweishun

Lee Plate

Creek

320

Capes Lake

REGIONAL DISTRICT OF COMOX STRATHCONA
REGIONAL DISTRICT OF ALBERNI CLAYOQUOT

See Map E3

See Map E4

See Map D4

93

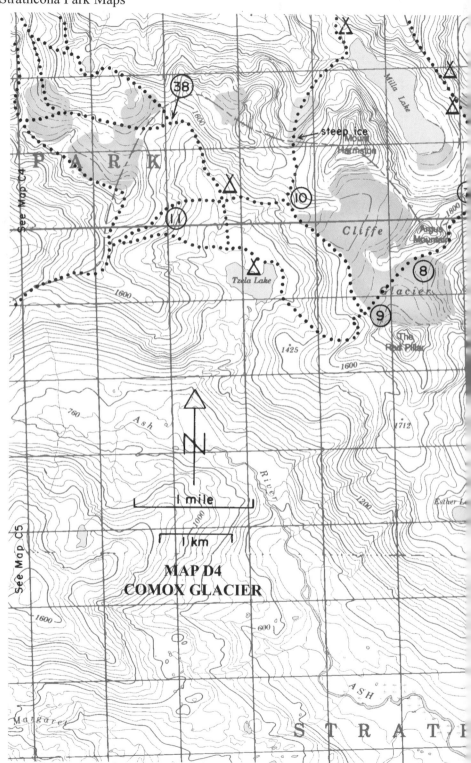

MAP D4
COMOX GLACIER

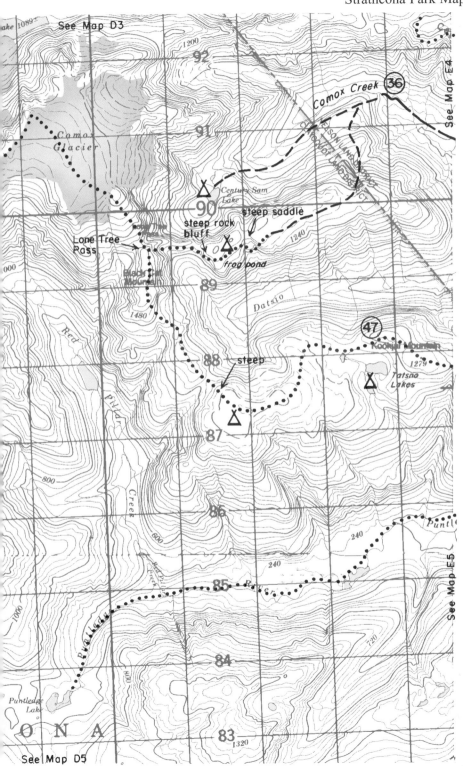

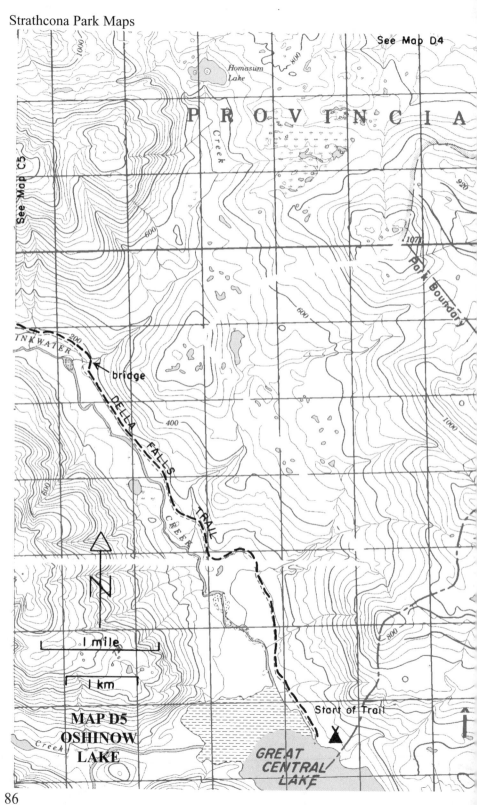

See Map D4

See Map C5

P R O V I N C I A

Homasum Lake

Creek

Park Boundary

INKWATER

bridge

DELLA FALLS TRAIL

CREEK

N

1 mile

1 km

MAP D5
OSHINOW
LAKE

Creek

Start of Trail

GREAT
CENTRAL
LAKE

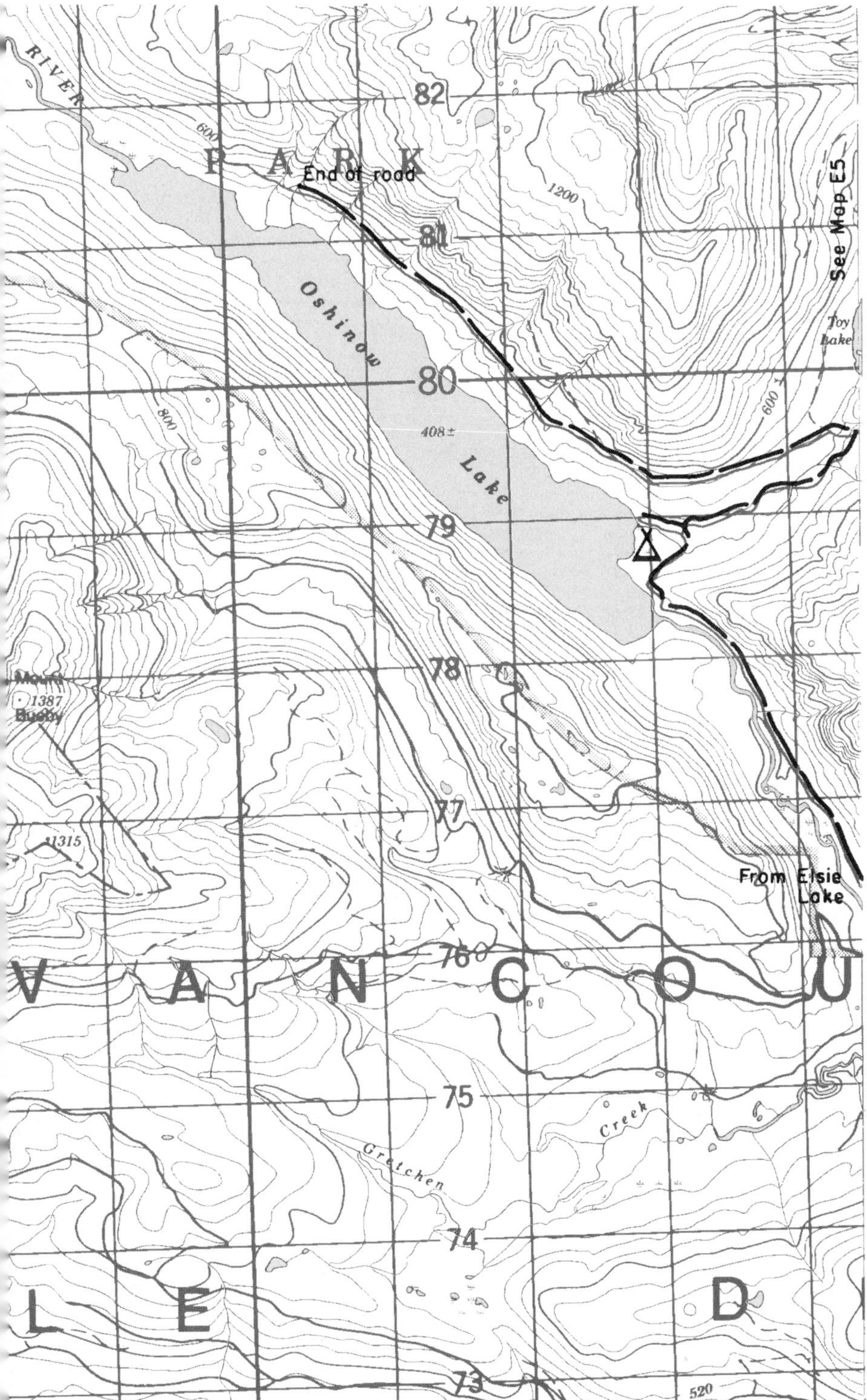
RIVER
600
P A R K
End of road
1200
82
81
See Map E5
Toy Lake
Oshinow
80
800
408±
Lake
600
79
78
Mount
1387
Busby
77
1315
From Elsie Lake
76
V A N C O U
75
Creek
Gretchen
74
L E D
73
520

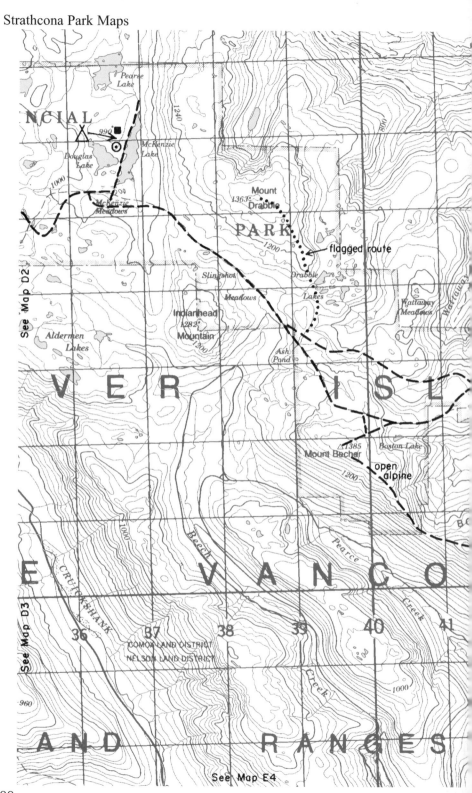

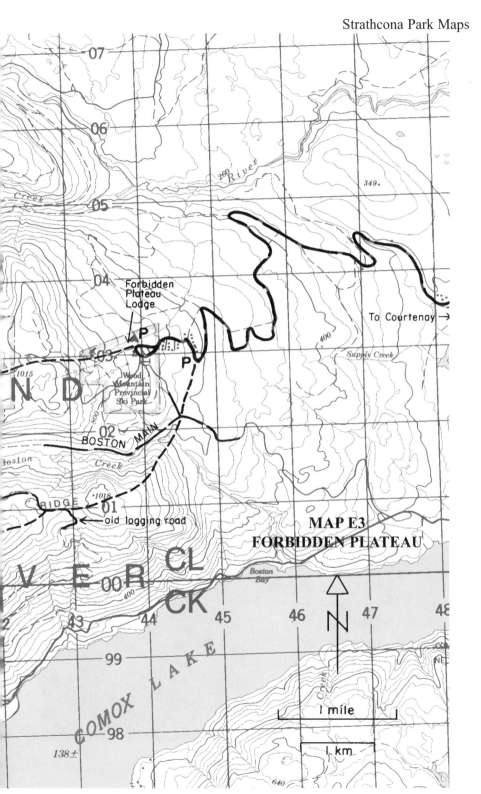

07

06

260 River

349.

05

Creek

04 Forbidden
Plateau
Lodge

To Courtenay →

P

03 P

400

Supply Creek

N D 1015

Wood
Mountain
Provincial
Ski Park

02 400
BOSTON MAIN

Boston Creek

1018

RIDGE 01
← old logging road

MAP E3
FORBIDDEN PLATEAU

V E 00 R CL
400 Boston
Bay

CK 45 46 N 47 48
43 44

99 L A K E

COMOX LAKE

98

138±

1 mile

1 km

640

Buttle Lake and Mount Albert Edward
from the top of Marble Meadows Trail

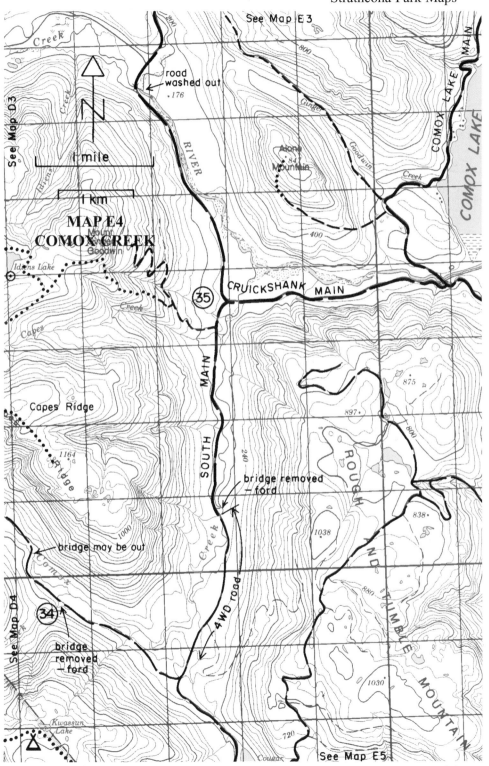

See Map E3

road washed out
.176

Creek

RIVER

Ginger

Alone Mountain
.84

Goodwin

Creek

COMOX LAKE MAIN

COMOX LAKE

See Map D3

Itkus

Creek

N
1 mile
1 km

**MAP E4
COMOX CREEK**

Mount Goodwin

Idens Lake

Capes

Creek

③⑤

CRUICKSHANK MAIN

400

800

Capes Ridge

1164

Ridge

1000

875

897.

800

ROUGH

bridge removed — ford

1038

838.

bridge may be out

Comox

SOUTH MAIN

Creek

790

AND TUMBLE

880

See Map D4

③④

bridge removed — ford

4WD road

1030

MOUNTAIN

720

Kwassun Lake

Cougar

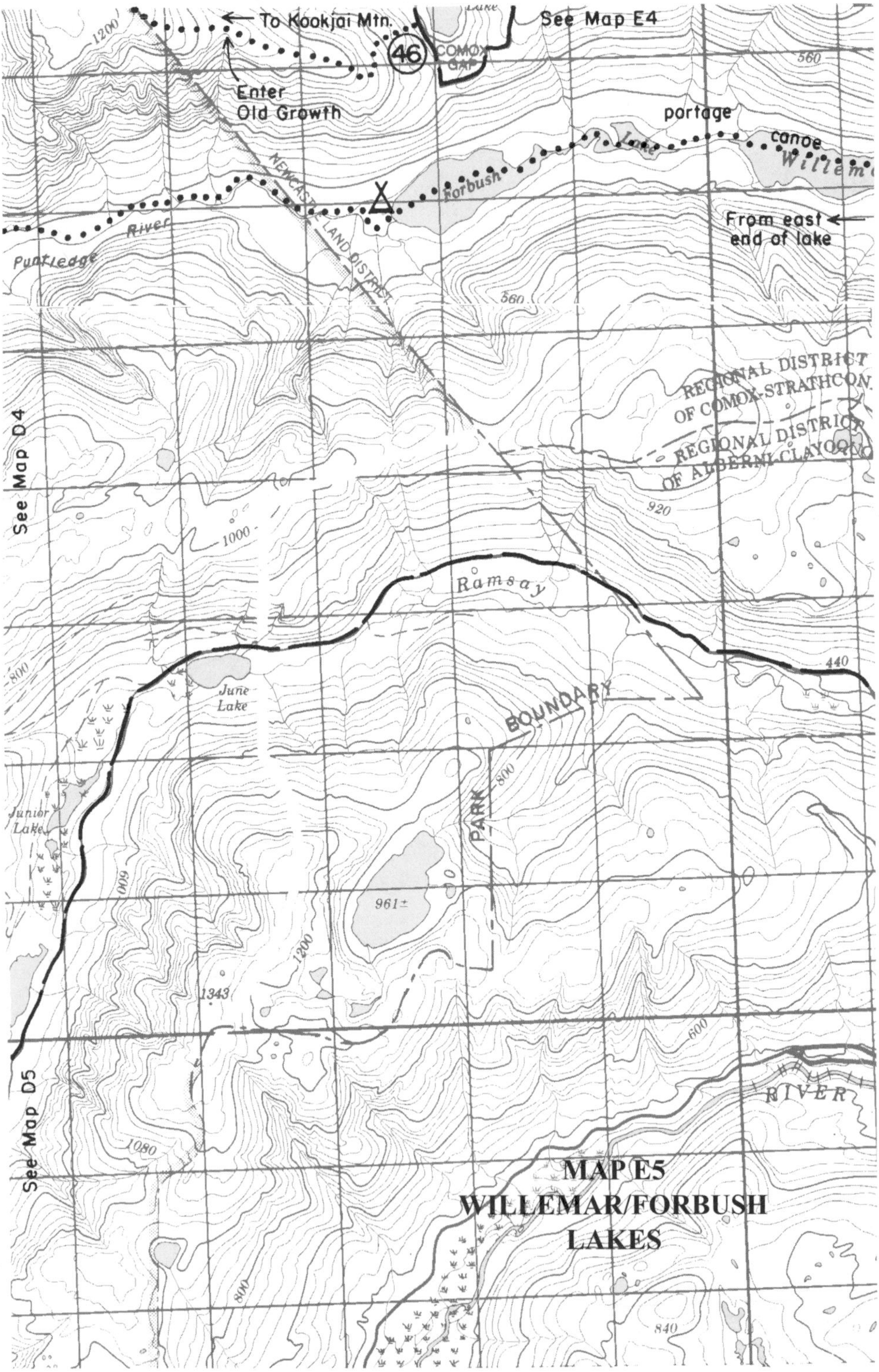

To Kookjai Mtn.

See Map E4

46

COMOX GAP

Enter
Old Growth

portage

canoe

Willem

Forbush

From east
end of lake

Puntledge

River

NEW ALAND DISTRICT

REGIONAL DISTRICT
OF COMOX-STRATHCONA

REGIONAL DISTRICT
OF ALBERNI CLAYOQUOT

Ramsay

See Map D4

1000

920

440

June
Lake

BOUNDARY

Junior
Lake

PARK

961±

1343

1200

See Map D5

600

RIVER

1080

MAP E5
WILLEMAR/FORBUSH
LAKES

840

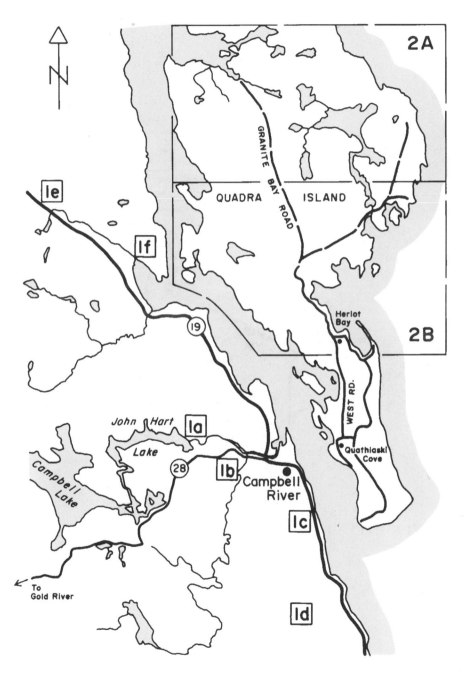

MAP 1
CAMPBELL RIVER AREA GENERAL MAP

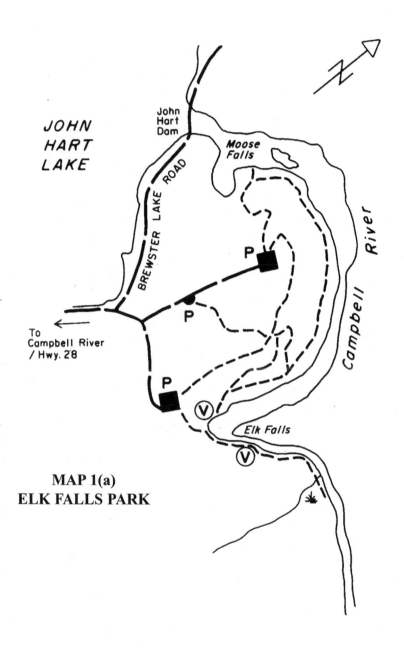

JOHN
HART
LAKE

John
Hart
Dam

Moose
Falls

BREWSTER LAKE ROAD

Campbell River

P

P

To
Campbell River
/ Hwy. 28

P

(V)

Elk Falls

(V)

**MAP 1(a)
ELK FALLS PARK**

AREAS OTHER THAN STRATHCONA PARK

TRAILS IN THE CAMPBELL RIVER AREA

At one time a handy booklet was available describing a variety of day hikes in the Campbell River and Quadra Island areas. This booklet now seems to be unavailable so a selection of these hikes and walks have been included in this book.

The Outdoor Recreation Council of BC produces a 1:100,000 scale (1cm = 1 km) recreation map of the Campbell River region, showing much useful information. This map covers the area north of Strathcona Park as far as Sayward, and is available at most sporting goods stores.

Very useful maps are available at no charge from the Forest Service offices and also from forest industry companies. See page 11.

(a) Elk Falls Park Trails (Map 1(a), page 94)

This series of trails is accessible from Elk Falls Provincial Park, located about 7 km from Campbell River on Highway 28 to Gold River. Turn off the highway at the top of "General Hill", cross a wooden bridge (the road to the left provides a view of the dam) to a fork in the road. The road to the right has a parking lot that overlooks the falls; the road on the left features groves of big timber. The main trail is approximately 2 km long, is quite steep in some sections and can be slippery during rainy periods. It takes 45 minutes for a round trip.

The trail follows the Campbell River from Moose Falls to Elk Falls, providing a beautiful walk through an area with gigantic Douglas-fir and cedar trees, some of which are 800 years old, and views of the numerous pools along the river course. The lookout provides a scenic view of Elk Falls, where the water falls some 50 m to the bottom and into Elk Falls canyon. The trail that follows the south side of the canyon is more difficult, with drops along this part of the canyon edge of almost 100 m.

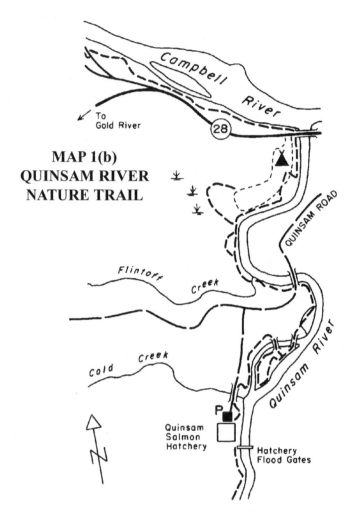

**MAP 1(b)
QUINSAM RIVER
NATURE TRAIL**

(b) Quinsam River Nature Trail

The trailhead is under the Quinsam River bridge, approximately 3.9 km towards Gold River from downtown Campbell River. This trail follows the Quinsam River for 3.3 km to the salmon hatchery, and a round trip takes about 2 hours. It is in good condition and provides an easy walk through a beautiful area. During the spawning season, salmon can be seen returning up the river. A campsite near the highway provides drinking water and toilet facilities. Another section of this trail follows the south bank of the Campbell River for 1.2 km to the power station.

(c) Beaver Lodge Lands Trails (Map 1(c), page 98)

This large area on the west side of Campbell River, and adjacent to new subdivisions, is being developed by the Forest Service for recreation. At present, trails are multiple-use and accommodate hikers, horses, runners and mountain bikers. These trails vary in skill level and character, but are mostly "easy" for hikers.

The area is accessed from Trask Road, Rockland Road, the north end of McPhedron Road and the Elk River Timber (ERT) Mainline.

These lands are undergoing a planning process, and therefore the current trail layout will have some changes, including more structures such as bridges and benches being put into place. The area is generally wet and muddy in winter, and new trail work over the next few years will improve drainage and trail surfaces.

The trail along **Simms Creek** has long been popular, and there are a number of ways to incorporate it into a circular tour from any of the area's access points. It takes about two hours to walk a round trip. Though generally in good condition and with a well-packed surface, it can be muddy in the rainy season.

The Simms Creek trail is an even-grade trail, providing an easy walk suitable for most users. At one point there is a view of swamp life, and the trail system provides an interesting variety of flora and fauna.

(d) Willow Creek Nature Trust Trails (Map 1(d), page 99)

Located at the southern end of the community of Campbell River, these trails are accessed from the Island Highway via Erickson Road, and also from Dahl or Martin Roads. They provide a beautiful walk along Willow Creek, a salmon enhancement stream. From a parking lot at Erickson Road the trail drops downhill to the stream. Turn east (left) and follow the streambank to an extension of Martin Road where you cross the stream on a log and return down the other bank. There are a number of interesting branch trails. The Willow Creek Watershed Society was started in the spring of 1995, and can be contacted through John Lewis (in Campbell River) at 287-2101.

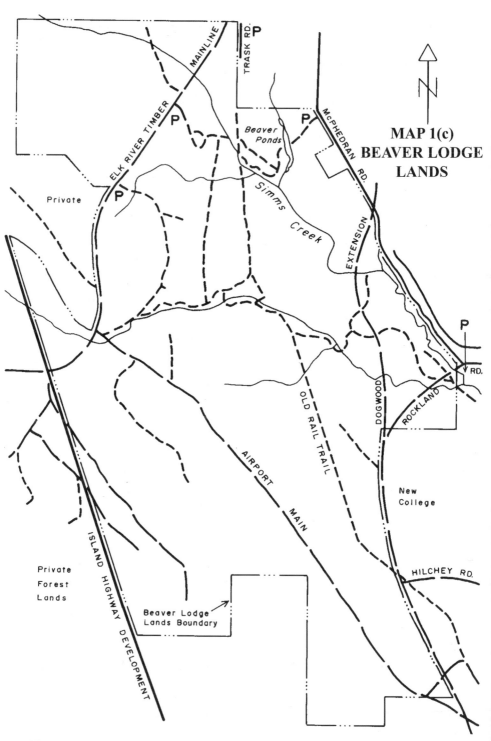

MAP 1(c)
BEAVER LODGE
LANDS

N

Beaver Ponds

Simms Creek

Private

Private
Forest
Lands

Beaver Lodge
Lands Boundary

New
College

HILCHEY RD.

TRASK RD.

ELK RIVER TIMBER

MAINLINE

McPHEDRAN RD.

EXTENSION

DOGWOOD

ROCKLAND

RD.

OLD RAIL TRAIL

AIRPORT MAIN

ISLAND HIGHWAY DEVELOPMENT

98

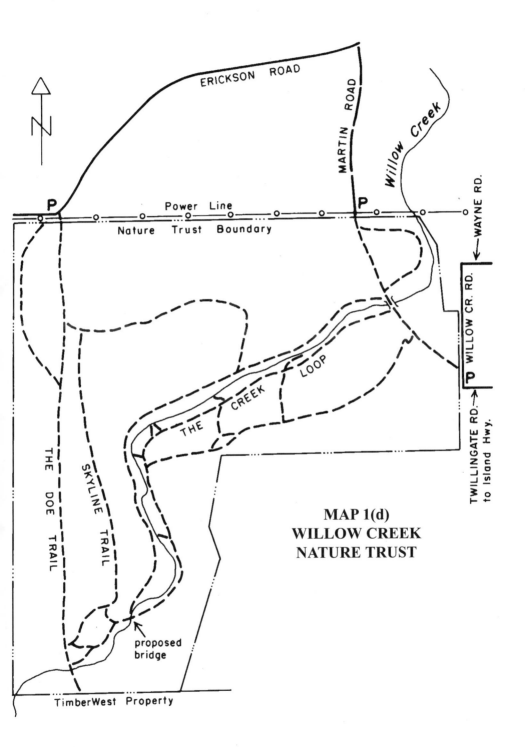

ERICKSON ROAD

MARTIN ROAD

Willow Creek

WAYNE RD.

P

Power Line

Nature Trust Boundary

P

WILLOW CR. RD.

P

TWILLINGATE RD.

to Island Hwy.

LOOP

THE CREEK

THE DOE TRAIL

SKYLINE TRAIL

N

proposed
bridge

MAP 1(d)
WILLOW CREEK
NATURE TRUST

TimberWest Property

99

MAP 1(e) MENZIES MOUNTAIN

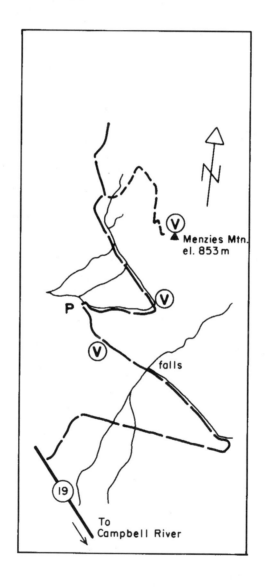

(e) Menzies Mountain Trail (Map 1(e), page 100)

Accessible off Highway 19, approximately 25.6 km north of Campbell River towards Sayward. The turnoff to the trail is on the east side of the highway. Currently (1995) active logging in the area means that the road can be driven as far as the second lookout, although caution should be taken during work hours and right of way given to logging trucks. This is a narrow gravel road with not many pullouts. The parking area has room for 4 or 5 vehicles.

This strenuous rocky trail has some steep sections. It provides spectacular views in all directions, especially of the mountains of Vancouver Island. Plan on 2 hours return from where you park.

(f) Ripple Rock Trail (Map 1(f), page 102)

Ripple Rock Trail is a 1½-2 hour walk (one way) leading to the Seymour Narrows lookout and views across to Quadra and Maud Islands. The marked trailhead is 15.5 km north of Campbell River with a parking pull-off on the east side of the highway.

The trail is 4 km long, with an easy to moderate grade to Menzies Bay and a steep section to Wilfred Point. It passes through areas which were logged about 70 years ago and now have Douglas-fir, red alder, broadleaf maple and western hemlock. On the east side of Menzies Creek the trail passes through two small patches of old growth with 300-year-old Sitka spruce and Douglas-fir.

There are good viewpoints along the trail and a nice sandy beach at Nymphe Cove. The trail was constructed in 1983 through a grant sponsored by the Campbell River Rotary Club.

Midway between the lookout and Maud Island is the site of the infamous Ripple Rock, two menacing rock pinnacles whose summits used to provide only a few metres clearance at low tide. This notorious marine hazard caused damage to dozens of ships and claimed 114 lives, resulting in a project to destroy Ripple Rock by blowing it to pieces. In 1958, the largest man-made, non-nuclear explosion in history reduced the rock by 370,000 tonnes to create a clearance of 13 m; however, in 1984, a cruise ship was holed off Maud Island and, although it limped to Duncan Bay, it sank at the dock.

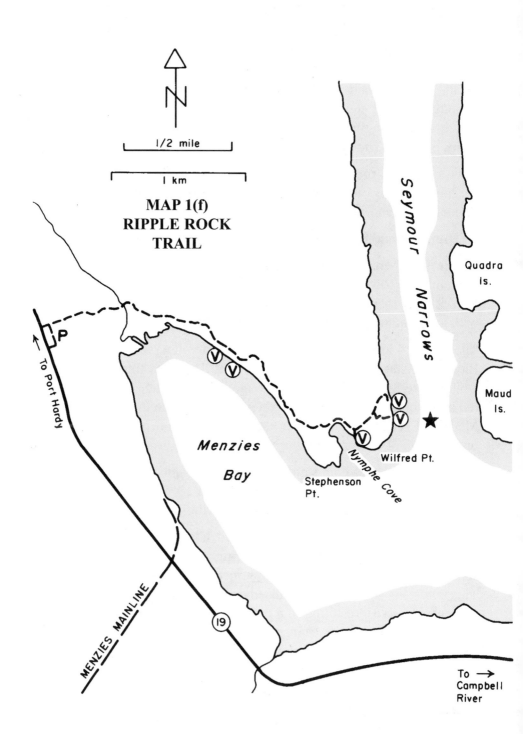

N

1/2 mile

1 km

**MAP 1(f)
RIPPLE ROCK
TRAIL**

Seymour Narrows

Quadra
Is.

Maud
Is.

P

To Port Hardy

*Menzies
Bay*

Wilfred Pt.

Nymphe Cove

Stephenson
Pt.

MENZIES MAINLINE

19

To →
Campbell
River

QUADRA ISLAND

Quadra Island is a short ferry ride across Discovery Passage from Campbell River. Here, just over two hundred years ago, Captain Vancouver made contact with the aboriginal people. He sent yawls (a type of small boat) through Discovery Passage before he brought in his ship, "Discovery", and anchored off Cape Mudge. Today the village of We-Wai-kai offers visitors a modern museum displaying outstanding examples of aboriginal art, returned from Ottawa where they had been held since confiscated by the RCMP in 1921.

The island offers many recreational opportunities including coastal kayaking, diving and fishing, lake canoeing and kayaking, and hiking. Although some trails are long-established, others have only been made recently, and many are former logging grades. On Quadra, as throughout BC, choices are being made as to how and where recreational opportunities, such as trails, will be developed.

The trails and routes described below are located in the northern central part of Quadra Island, with road distances measured from Heriot Bay store. All the *trails* are maintained by the BC Forest Service, and are well signed. *Routes*, which are passable ways that may not be maintained or signed, are usually only suitable for experienced hikers.

Generally these trails and routes are located on Crown land which is managed by the Ministry of Forests and/or TimberWest, the forest company holding Tree Farm License (TFL) #47. We acknowledge their assistance and co-operation in constructing these trails. The kindness of private-land owners, in permitting trails and routes over their land, is also very much appreciated.

Noel Lax, and fellow hikers of Quadra Island

103

MORTE LAKE AREA

From Heriot Bay, take the Hyacinthe Bay Road for 6 km and turn west on Walcan Road for 700 m to the main parking area for Morte Lake Trail.

(a) Morte Lake Trail - south shore loop

A pleasant forest hike of 7.2 km with good views of Morte Lake, the southwest slopes of Chinese Mountains and glimpses of the mountains of Vancouver Island. Travelling in a counter-clockwise direction the trail follows a gentle incline above McKercher Creek for 2.3 km to the east end of Morte Lake, which takes about 30 minutes. This trail is a popular fishing path to Morte Lake. Stay to the left at the fork just before the lake, and follow the trail to a small marshy area (bridged) by a sandy beach at the southernmost end of the lake. The trail rises again over rock ridges before dropping steeply to Mud Lake. At times the Mud Lake and Reed Lake sections can be wet, and if so the Walcan Road can be easily accessed from the west end of each of these lakes. Allow about 2 hours.

(b) Morte Lake Trail - north shore

Access is as above but stay to the right at the fork before Morte Lake and follow the trail around the lake. This is a more strenuous section and the 3 km will take about an hour. At the west end of Morte Lake the trail crosses Quadra Conservancy property: please respect it by staying on the trail.

NORTH AND SOUTH CHINESE MOUNTAINS AREA

Chinese Mountain Road is 6.7 km from Heriot Bay and 700 m north of Walcan Road.

The trail to the North Peak is easier, but the view from the South Peak is far more spectacular with a panorama of the Coast Range, Desolation Sound, islands, inlets, the Strait of Georgia and the Vancouver Island Mountains. Moss-covered rock ridges and weather-worn stunted growth provide both peaks with a subalpine characteristic at only 250-300 m of elevation.

Chinese Mountains area has a particular reputation for ticks, in season. Check carefully after a hike that you haven't gained such an unwanted friend.

(c) South and North Peak Trails

From the Chinese Mountain Road parking area take the left-hand (west) trail around the base of the mountain. After about 500 m keep right, uphill, at the signed fork. (The trail going down is a short connection to Morte Lake Trail). The path leading to the viewpoint cairn is well marked and, on the ridge, passes a fork which leads down the east side of South Peak, permitting a round trip. Allow 2-4 hours for this 2.7 km loop.

Alternatively, to reach the South Peak from its east side, take the right-hand (east) trail from the parking area up a fairly steep old logging road. At the signed fork, just where the incline eases, go left. Once on the south summit ridge this trail joins the trail coming up from the west side (above) and continues to the lookout cairn.

For the North Peak, start as for the South Peak, east side (above) but keep straight on where the incline eases. (Note: when reaching the North Peak rock ridge from the trail, take particular note of your surroundings. It's easy to overshoot the trail on the way back, and then get lost. A sign has been installed, but this is no substitute for good backwoods skills.)

(d) West Chinese Mountain Ridge Route

A partially-marked route (not a trail), suitable only for experienced hikers, follows the southwest edge of a rock ridge extending from South Peak to West Peak by way of Beech's Mountain. This is a fairly strenuous hike over rock ridges and through old growth, reaching an elevation of 520 m. Allow 6 hours.

West Peak itself, having some open rock but lacking a focal point, is not particularly interesting, but the ridge-edge scramble certainly is, with constantly-unfolding views of Georgia Strait, Quadra Island and Morte Lake, as well as Vancouver Island's peaks to the west. The route is little used at present with no worn trail to follow, and because of dog-leg changes in direction it is easy to get off-route.

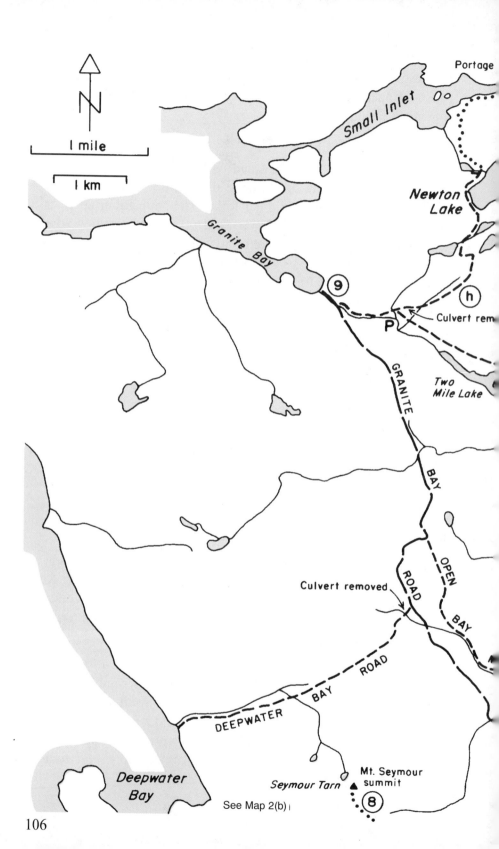

Portage

Small Inlet

Newton Lake

Granite Bay

⑨

ⓗ

P

Culvert rem

GRANITE

Two Mile Lake

BAY

OPEN

Culvert removed

ROAD

BAY

DEEPWATER

BAY

ROAD

Deepwater Bay

Seymour Tarn

Mt. Seymour summit

⑧

See Map 2(b)

1 mile

1 km

Waiatt Bay

MAP 2(a)
QUADRA ISLAND (north)

Nameless
Lake

Clear
Lake

Portage
route

Little
Main
Lake

Main Lake

Mine
Lake

Stramberg Cr.

⑧

⑨

Stramberg
Lake

⑨

SURGE NARROWS RD.

Village Bay
Lake

See Map 2(b)

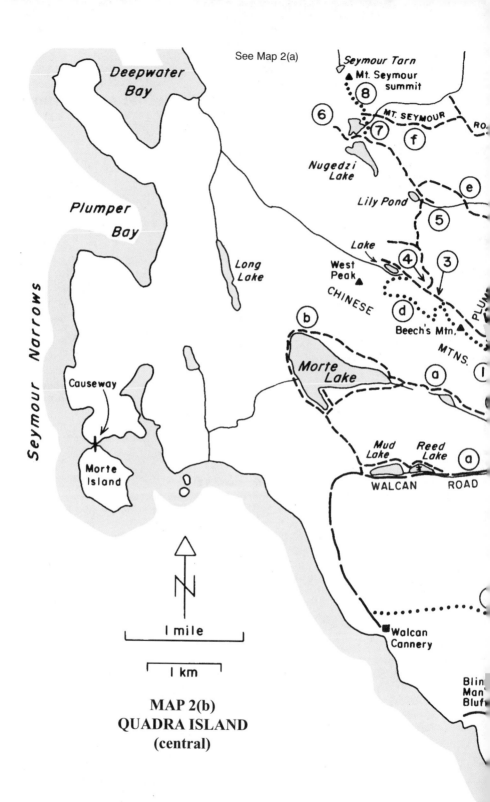

See Map 2(a)

MAP 2(b)
QUADRA ISLAND
(central)

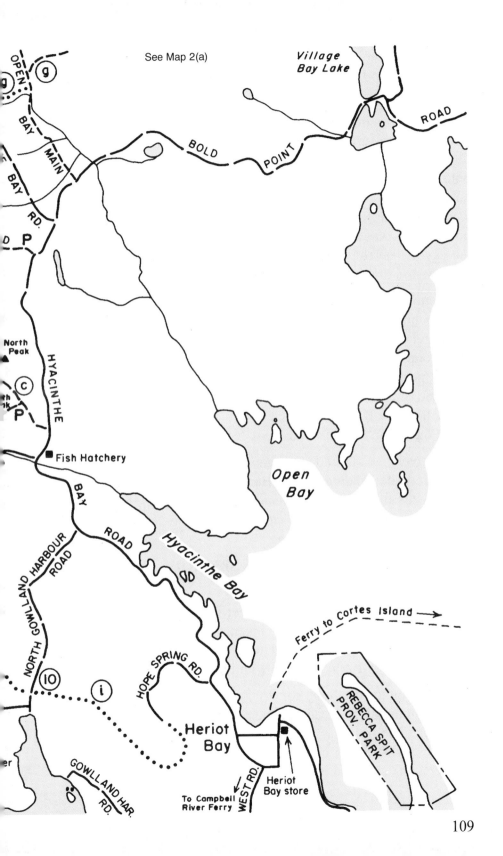

See Map 2(a)

Village Bay Lake

ROAD

BOLD POINT

g

OPEN BAY MAIN

BAY RD.

P

North Peak

c

P

HYACINTHE

■ Fish Hatchery

Open Bay

BAY ROAD

NORTH GOWLLAND HARBOUR ROAD

Hyacinthe Bay

Ferry to Cortes Island →

REBECCA SPIT PROV. PARK

10

i

HOPE SPRING RD.

Heriot Bay

GOWLLAND HAR. RD.

WEST RD.

To Campbell River Ferry

■ Heriot Bay store

If you do, keep high on the line of the ridge edge and you should again see cairns.

This route commences after taking the trail up the west side of South Peak to just below a saddle (where the trail leaves the old logging grade for a second time and goes up worn earthen steps onto bedrock) at a sign to "South Peak Lookover". [1] The route heads northwest below the saddle and dense second growth, and is well marked at first with cairns and flagging. After passing a large boulder the route drops into bush, rises and then forks. Keep left to the skyline on ridge bedrock. (The right fork [2] leads to a cut-off route across the ridge to Plumper Bay Road.)

Continuing over Beech's Mountain the main route intercepts another link trail [3] from the brow of a steep hill on Plumper Bay Road and continues along the ridge edge to a logging road. Bearing right, loop back to the Plumper Bay Road (southeast 750 m, a fork to the north leads to Nugedzi Lakes and Mount Seymour and continue straight down past a steep rough section to the "big bend", where the cut-off route to South Peak starts on an old skidder road to the right (south). This leads back to the fork above.

Alternatively, go 100 m farther down Plumper Bay Road to a small rise before descending again. Here another route [4] on the right (south) cuts through the trees and follows rock ridges around the northeast side of a timbered cirque to join the North Peak Trail, which leads to the parking area.

NUGEDZI LAKES AND MOUNT SEYMOUR
(e) Nugedzi Lakes Trail

This 4.25-km trail begins with a rather boring 45-minute grunt up an old logging road. However, hikers are well rewarded by the high, mossy and beautiful ancient forest and charming Nugedzi Lakes, especially Little Nugedzi with its bonsai-like islets.

Take Hyacinthe Bay Road for 9.1 km from Heriot Bay, then turn left on Plumper Bay Road (signposted Nugedzi Lakes) to parking 100 m in. The trail was developed in 1991 by the Quadra Island Recreation Society in conjunction with Fletcher Challenge (now TimberWest) Ltd., and is well marked. Allow 4½ hours.

A spur trail branches at the "Lily Pond", either south [5] to a lookover (half hour return) or west to a route connecting with Plumper Bay Road and Chinese Mountains. Beyond Nugedzi Lake another spur trail rises to a viewpoint [6] overlooking Discovery Passage (allow 1 hour return from the bridge). At the east end of the lake-edge boardwalk at Little Nugedzi (which provides access for naturalists to study and enjoy the lake/marsh transition zone) there is a 500 m link [7] to the Mount Seymour Road.

Alternatively (probably an easier, more pleasant access), take the Mount Seymour Road (see below) and a short link trail (see map) to Little Nugedzi Lake.

(f) Mount Seymour Route

At 650 m (2,019 ft), Mount Seymour is the highest elevation on Quadra Island. Openings in the old growth provide segmented viewscapes, though the debris from logging near the summit causes some sadness.

A little more than 9 km from Heriot Bay, take the Granite Bay Road for 2 km to Mount Seymour Road on the left. It's a rough road even for 4-wheel-drives so park at the side of Granite Bay Road. On the walk in, keep left at a fork near the half-way point. A sign 100 m east of the connector trail to Little Nugedzi Lake marks the start of the Mount Seymour summit route. Follow cairns and flagging but be prepared for sharp changes in direction. Just beyond the summit a game trail drops through old growth to a delightful small tarn. Allow 4-5 hours for the round trip to the summit.

NORTHEAST QUADRA ISLAND

(g) Stramberg Lake Route

This route is an easy and fairly shady walk in the woods along the east side of, or right around, a tranquil and as-yet-unspoiled lake, with vistas towards Mount Seymour.

On the other side of Granite Bay Road from the Mount Seymour trailhead, an eastwards route provides a link to Stramberg Lake and the chain of Little Main, Main, Mine and Village Bay Lakes. Follow down and along a creek leading to Open Bay Main. Go north on this road for 600 m and take the fork to the right. Always bearing left, go 250 m beyond the first view of and access to the lake, then left on an old skidder road (may be signed). A good route follows the lakeshore to a beaver dam beyond the north end of the lake. (Some route-finding may be necessary through an alder bottom to avoid going through wetland grass). Allow 4½ hours for this east side return.

A circuit of the lake can be made by crossing Stramberg Creek on logs below the abandoned beaver dam [8]. Pick up a skidder road 15 m beyond the creek, bearing left to return to Open Bay Main. Since removal of a culvert it may at times be difficult to cross Canyon Creek. Just below the ford there is a nice waterfall and a small canyon, which are worth a short detour. Allow 4-6 hours for a round trip.

(h) Newton Lake Trail/Small Inlet Route

This hike begins as a fairly easy forest trail passing other lakes on the way to Newton Lake. Beyond, a more strenuous route follows an old prospectors' trail down to a promontory in Small Inlet, then links with an old portage route (can be wet) to Waiatt Bay. With only informal consent, this route crosses private property belonging to TimberWest and Merrill & Ring Timber. Please respect this and do not light fires or camp in this area.

Follow Granite Bay Road north to within 200 m of Granite Bay, and at the sign [9] turn right onto a rough road for 600 m to a fork. Stay left for this trailhead. Allow 2 hours return to Newton Lake and 4½ hours return to Waiatt Bay.

The fork to the right is the old logging grade to Clear Lake. This is now impassable to vehicles but it makes a good hike past Two Mile Lake.

TRAIL CONNECTIONS BETWEEN HERIOT BAY AND MORTE LAKE

These are gentle forest hikes with the potential to link the south end of Quadra with trail system described above. At present, direct public access from Heriot Bay is possible but difficult, except for a route (being developed as this is written) from the top end of Hope Spring Road (1.4 km from Heriot Bay). Meanwhile, access is from the north via North Gowlland Harbour Road (4.7 km from Heriot Bay.)

(i) Old Gowlland Harbour Trail

This trail (technically a route, but named a trail) starts on the creek side, about 200 m up the road [10] from the gate to a log-sorting ground. Except under the wettest conditions the creek is passable on stepping stones. The trail starts in a southeasterly direction, and then curves to join Hope Spring Road. At the height of land above North Gowlland Harbour Road, open bluffs to the west offer good views over Discovery Passage and Gowlland Harbour. Allow 2-3 hours return.

(j) Missing Link Trail

Also technically a route, this trail starts as a bush road on the west side of North Gowlland Harbour Road about 150 m from the sorting ground gate, almost opposite the end of Old Gowlland Harbour Trail. After 700 m., stay left at a fork and go up and over a hill. (A side trip to the south, involving some bush-bashing, offers worthwhile views from a prominent bluff, sometimes called Blind Man's Bluff). The main trail comes out near the cannery, from which Walcan Road leads north to Morte Lake and Hyacinthe Bay Road. Allow 2-3 hours return.

Note: The route enters Walcan's private property by verbal consent only. Please respect this, particularly when parking, as large tractor trailers use this road at all hours.

SNOWDEN DEMONSTRATION FOREST

The Snowden Demonstration Forest was designed to raise public awareness about Integrated Resource Management in provincial forests. In this "active" forest, silvicultural systems are integrated with other forest interests including recreation. An extensive system of trails in this area, while perhaps not for the purist or those who prefer alpine hiking, provides a variety of interpretive and recreational forest-based opportunities suitable for all ages. Mountain bikes are allowed on the trails.

This area is just 16.5 km from Campbell River. Take the turnoff to Elk Falls Provincial Park on the right, 7 km along Highway 28 to Gold River. At the sign for Loveland Bay stay left and cross the John Hart Dam. Follow directional signs from there.

Interpretive Trails:

Three hiking trails are located on Snowden Road:

- **Old Forest Trail:** 325 m long, a 15 min. walk through an old growth forest.

- **Ecosystem Trail:** 800 m., shows examples of forest ecology.

- **Silviculture Trail:** 1.1 km. The complete forest management cycle is examined, from site preparation to planting, tending and harvesting

Detailed handouts are available from the Forest Service office in Campbell River.

Recreational Trails:

Numerous trails provide opportunities for hiking, cycling, running and mushroom picking.

Frog Lake Trail System

(1) Old Rail Trail: 4.2 km along a historical rail grade. The trailhead is located north of Elmer Lake on the Frog Lake Road.

(2) Lookout Loop: 3.2 km. The loop starts from the Frog Lake Road, climbing up and over rocky outcrops, then down through forest and wetland areas. It joins up with the Old Rail Trail.

(3) Enchanted Forest: 4.3 km through lush forest and along rough gravel roads. Cyclists are recommended to ride this loop in a clockwise direction.

(4) Riley Lake Connector: 1.9 km of forest trail and old rail grade that connects Enchanted Forest and Lost Lake Trails.

Headbanger Hookup: Principally for cyclists.

Lost Lake Trail System

(5) Lost Lake Trail: 5.5 km loop with picnic tables at the south end of the lake. Short hike to rocky viewpoint.

(6) Mudhoney Pass: Principally for cyclists.

(7) The Lost Frog: 8.2 km of almost continuous rail grade, with a few rougher connections. Access is via the north end of Devlin Road or Frog Lake Road.

(8) Frog Lake Road: 5.7 km, an optional link between Frog Lake and Lost Lake trail systems.

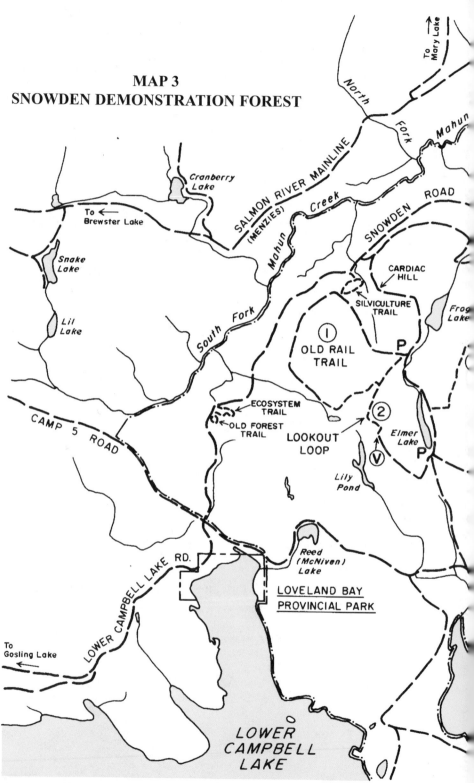

MAP 3
SNOWDEN DEMONSTRATION FOREST

To Mary Lake

North Fork Mahun

SALMON RIVER MAINLINE (MENZIES)

Mahun Creek

SNOWDEN ROAD

Cranberry Lake

To Brewster Lake

Snake Lake

Lil Lake

South Fork

CARDIAC HILL

SILVICULTURE TRAIL

Frog Lake

P

① OLD RAIL TRAIL

ECOSYSTEM TRAIL

OLD FOREST TRAIL

LOOKOUT LOOP

②

Elmer Lake

P

CAMP 5 ROAD

Ⓥ

Lily Pond

Reed (McNiven) Lake

LOVELAND BAY PROVINCIAL PARK

LOWER CAMPBELL LAKE RD.

To Gosling Lake

LOWER CAMPBELL LAKE

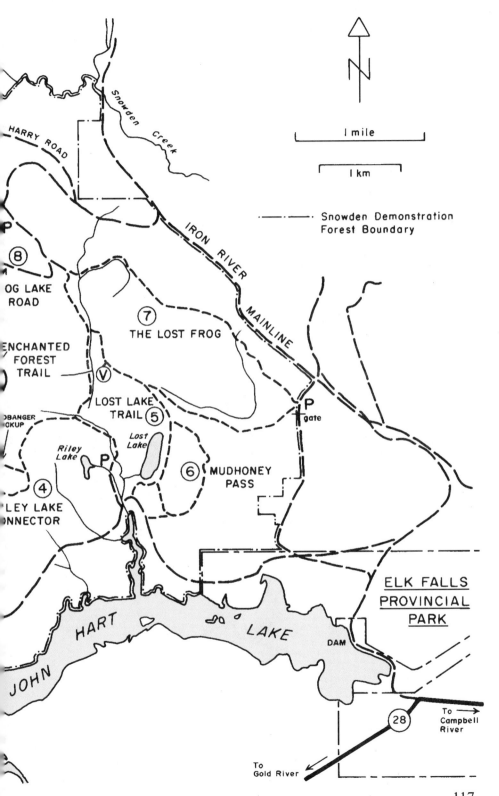

N

| 1 mile |
| 1 km |

—·—·— Snowden Demonstration
Forest Boundary

HARRY ROAD

Snowden Creek

IRON RIVER MAINLINE

P

⑧

OG LAKE
ROAD

⑦
THE LOST FROG

ENCHANTED
FOREST
TRAIL

Ⓥ

LOST LAKE
TRAIL ⑤

OBANGER
ICKUP

Riley
Lake

P

Lost
Lake

P
gate

⑥ MUDHONEY
PASS

④

LEY LAKE
ONNECTOR

ELK FALLS
PROVINCIAL
PARK

JOHN HART LAKE

DAM

㉘

To →
Campbell
River

To
Gold River

117

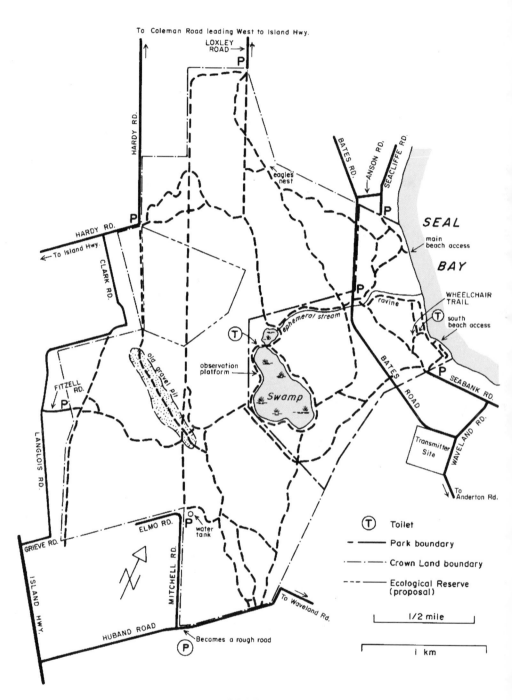

MAP 4
SEAL BAY REGIONAL NATURE PARK

SEAL BAY REGIONAL NATURE PARK
(XWEE XWHWA LUQ)

XWEE XWHWA LUQ is a Salish name suggested by the Comox Band meaning "place with an atmosphere of peace and serenity".

Seal Bay Park is administered by Comox-Strathcona Regional District, and the Crown Land portion is the responsibility of the BC Forest Service. The trails were constructed 1971-1973 by the Comox-Strathcona Natural History Society with L.I.P. grant support.

Newcomers are recommended to access the park at Bates Road, via Anderton Road or Coleman Road. From the Comox junction in Courtenay, Coleman Road is 10.6 km.

SAYWARD FOREST

Named after William P. Sayward, a pioneer logger and sawmill operator in the area, the Sayward Forest is an undulating area largely covered with immature second growth timber, and with numerous lakes and creeks. In 1938 a large forest fire burned much of the area. It was subsequently replanted and today this is the most intensively managed forest in BC.

The BC Forest Service Recreation Program has developed rustic recreation sites throughout the area in conjunction with a continuous canoe and portage route. The Sayward Forest Canoe Route is included in this book as an interesting recreation opportunity that visitors to the area may wish to combine with hiking opportunities.

The canoe route is best accessed from Morton Lake Provincial Park. Turn off the North Island Highway (Highway 19) about 13 km north of Campbell River onto Menzies Bay Mainline.

A free brochure is available from the Forest Service giving route details and safety recommendations.

A circuit of this 11-lake system is approximately 40 km including about 7 km of portages. Most canoeists take about 3 to 4 days.

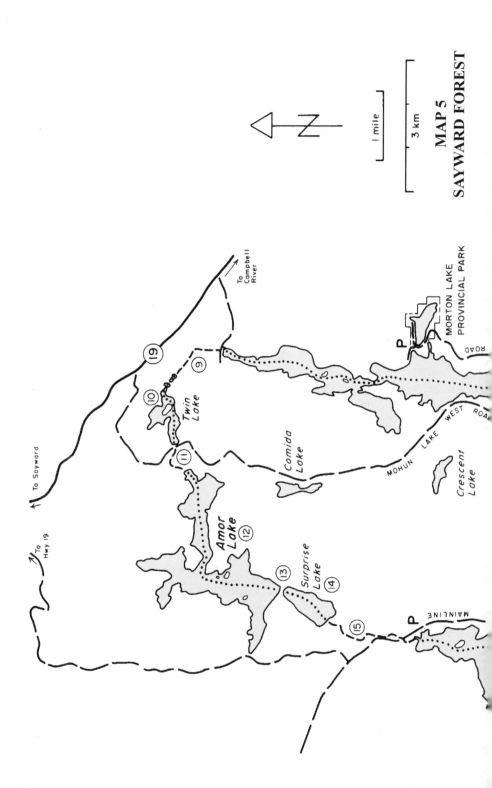

To Campbell River

19

9

10

Twin Lake

11

Comida Lake

Crescent Lake

MOHUN LAKE WEST ROAD

ROAD

MORTON LAKE
PROVINCIAL PARK

P

To Sayward

To Hwy.19

Amor Lake

12

13

Surprise Lake

14

15

P

MAINLINE

N

1 mile

3 km

MAP 5
SAYWARD FOREST

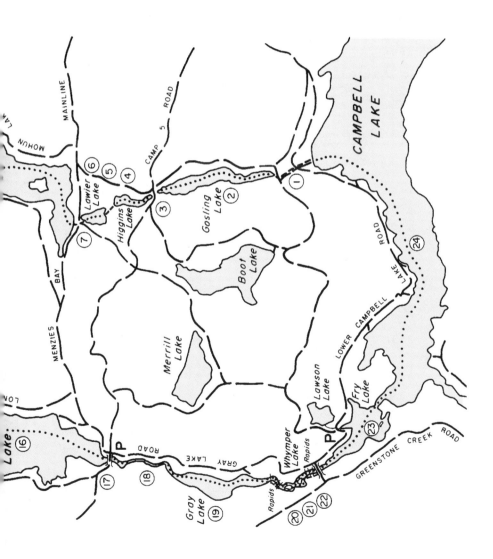

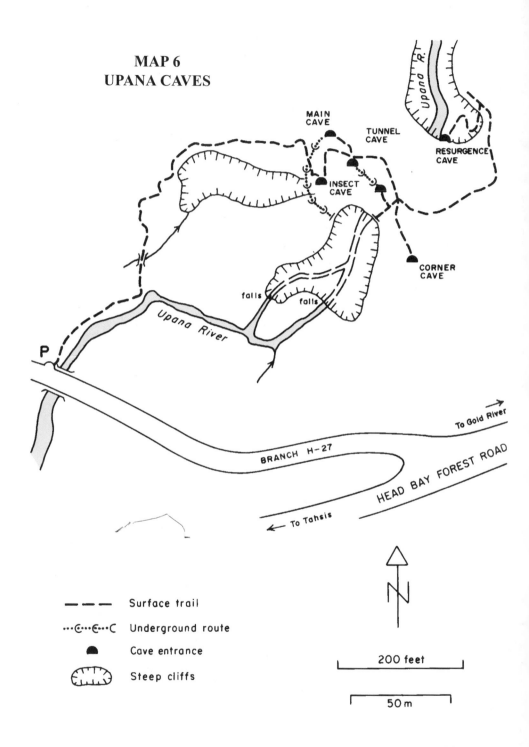

**MAP 6
UPANA CAVES**

Upana R.

MAIN
CAVE

TUNNEL
CAVE

RESURGENCE
CAVE

INSECT
CAVE

CORNER
CAVE

falls

falls

Upana River

P

To Gold River

BRANCH H-27

HEAD BAY FOREST ROAD

← To Tahsis

– – – Surface trail

···C···C···C Underground route

⬤ Cave entrance

Steep cliffs

N

200 feet

50 m

UPANA CAVES

The Upana Caves are located 17 km northwest of Gold River on the Head Bay Forest Road (to Tahsis). Driving time from Gold River is 25 minutes. The trail is included in this book because it is mostly a surface trail of about 400 m in a forest (replanted in 1981) setting, with the added interest of your being able to observe, and explore, a natural cave system. It is recommended that visitors pick up a self-guided tour brochure from a Forest Service office (Campbell River). These notes are taken from that brochure.

The first systematic exploration and mapping of these caves was undertaken in 1975 by recreational cavers. Cavers named the cave system after the Upana River, which flows through one of the caves. The cave interiors remain in a relatively wild, undeveloped state.

The Upana Caves are comprised of several individual caves ranging in size from single rooms to branching passages of varying length. There are 15 known entrances within the system, and the combined length of cave passages is approximately 450 m (1,476 ft).

To safely explore the caves you should carry a reliable flashlight or headlamp. A good light will help you to see the cave features and to watch your footing on uneven floors. The Upana Caves are a year-round experience. No matter what the weather is outside, the temperature inside the caves averages a chilly 7° Celsius, so bring a sweater or jacket.

It is very important that visitors be careful not to disturb the cave environment. Keep to the established trails and underground routes, do not touch delicate cave formations, and refrain from smoking and lighting fires.

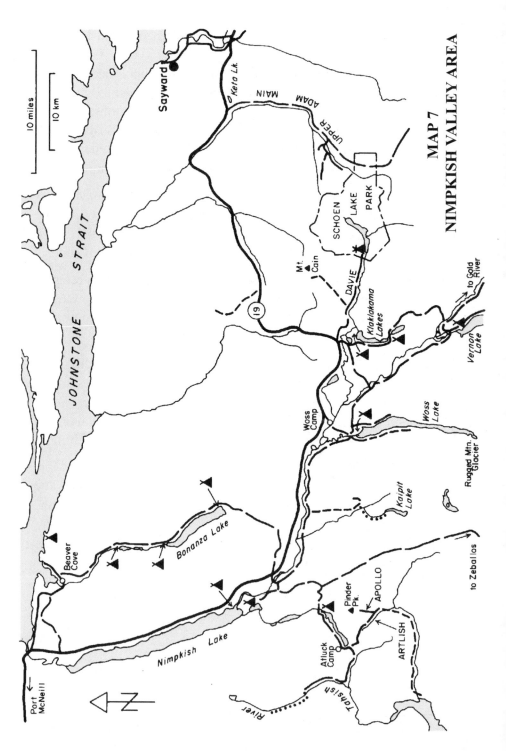

MAP 7
NIMPKISH VALLEY AREA

NIMPKISH VALLEY

When travelling north there are two routes to the Nimpkish Valley:

(a) from Campbell River and Sayward. Highway 19, paved all the way, enters the Nimpkish Valley near Klaklakama Lakes; or

(b) from Gold River by unpaved logging roads. The first 19 km are managed by Pacific Forest Products Ltd., and roughly the next 64 km by TimberWest Forest Ltd., to either Crowman Lake or Woss Lake where the roads connect with Highway 19.

The Regional District of Mount Waddington at Port McNeill and the appropriate logging companies (addresses on page 11) could also give you more local information. The Nimpkish watershed is all under Canadian Forest Products Ltd. (Canfor) Tree Farm Licence #37. Distances are marked along the Canfor Road at 10 km intervals starting from Nimpkish Camp southward. Please light fires only in designated campsites.

Pinder Peak by Atluck Lake is a rewarding challenge to strong hikers. This steep route can be accessed by boat across Atluck Lake, or via Artlish Main and Apollo, but a 4-wheel-drive vehicle is recommended. Check conditions beforehand.

Rugged Mountain, at the head of Woss Lake, is the highest peak in a compact and impressive group of peaks of interest to alpine climbers both in winter and summer. While traditional access to this area was by boat up Woss Lake, few parties enter this way today. Logging operations in the Nomash River valley to the west of Rugged Mountain have developed roads on the western side of the range almost to the very base of Rugged Mountain itself (via the heavily-eroded spur N20 in Nathan Creek). A steep hike and scramble from the upper part of this spur allows hikers to reach the main glacier in 3-4 hours. To go farther, experience in glacier travel is required.

Sandy Briggs

(a) Kaipit Lake Fire Trail (Map 7, page 124)

Part of the old fire access trail still exists, but is no longer maintained. This is suitable for strong hikers only. From Woss Lake recreational campsite, take the Canfor logging road to Nimpkish and about 18 km will bring you to the Kaipit turnoff. It's about

7 km to the trailhead where a difficult creek crossing must be made. The trail (now more a route than a trail) passes through beautiful but difficult terrain. If you wish to make this trip it is advisable to tell the Nimpkish Valley Search & Rescue Team of your plans (phone 974-5551).

(b) Tahsish River Trail (Map 7, page 124)

This is accessible at various points across the river from the logging road out of Atluck Camp. The trail is prettier upstream.

Trails Proposed

Canfor plans to construct a nature trail at Woss Lake recreational campsite and a trail in Mount Cain Regional Park when funding is possible.

SCHOEN LAKE PROVINCIAL PARK

The road bridge leading to the BC Parks campsite is being re-built. The new bridge should be decked and open in time for the 1996 season. Check with BC Parks at Miracle Beach (see page 11).

Canfor has constructed a road through this park in order to remove timber from beyond the south boundary of the park. The right-of-way for the road was identified in the Order-In-Council that established the park.

Access to Schoen Lake Campground

Obtain Canfor's recreational pamphlet. For Schoen Lake, going north on Highway 19, drive about 54 km from Sayward, and near Crowman Lake turn left onto road signposted "Mount Cain and Schoen Lake" (see Map 7, page 124). (If travelling from Woss, turn right about 20 km east of Woss.) Follow all signs to Schoen Lake Provincial Park (about 16 km) via Davie Road - a driveable gravel road but its final 3 km are in poor condition. Here you will find 10 developed campsites and a view, down the lake, of Mount Schoen.

(a) Schoen Creek Trail (Map 8, page 128)

(Hiking time to the end of the defined trail - 2 hours return, but, in 1995, the trail was overgrown and hard to follow.) The trail begins at the most-southerly camping spot of Schoen Lake's west shore campsite and is flagged with blue ribbons.

The Davie River is crossed via a secondary log jam, the main one being at the river's exit from the lake. Use caution on this trail river crossing. On the other side of the river the hemlock/balsam forest has an imposing primeval quality. Undergrowth is sparse and visibility through the trees is possible for 50 m and more. In the Schoen Creek delta, after a 10-minute walk from the trail's last brush with the lake shore, the hiker will reach the end of the defined trail and a route junction. To the east is a red-ribboned trail which quickly fades, but to the south is the blue-ribboned route heading up the Schoen Creek Valley. The valley route has been used for a while; on the east side of Schoen Creek old step-niched logs provide some brief easy walking.

From here strong hikers could pick their own route up to the saddle: eight hours steady hiking and well worth the effort.

(b) Nisnak Lake Trail (Map 8, page 129)

About a 5-km boat trip is involved to the head of the lake. Beware: the lake can be rough. The trail has not been maintained, and, in 1995, was overgrown and hard to find.

The trail starts from a natural landing site by a grove of big cedars [1] where three camping spots are possible. Marked by some old blazes and ribbons, it runs through a mature hemlock/spruce forest and is mostly well-defined on the south side of Nisnak Creek.

It climbs up on the bench above the creek valley and does not approach the creek until crossing it east of the large alder slide. The alder slide is a notable landmark, at least 200 m wide. Unfortunately, on the north side of the creek, the trail to Nisnak Lake (and also continuing eastwards from it) has many windfalls and is at times difficult to locate. Once through the windfalls the trail meanders through the meadows and isolated stands of timber. Here, it is very well-defined and has some muddy parts. From these meadows can be seen views of the five peaks of Mount Schoen and, though too distant to be impressive, Schoen Falls, below the fortress-like South Peak. This is moose pasture country without the moose.

Return hiking time from Schoen Lake to Upper Adam River: 4½ hours. Hiking time to meadows: 3 hours return.

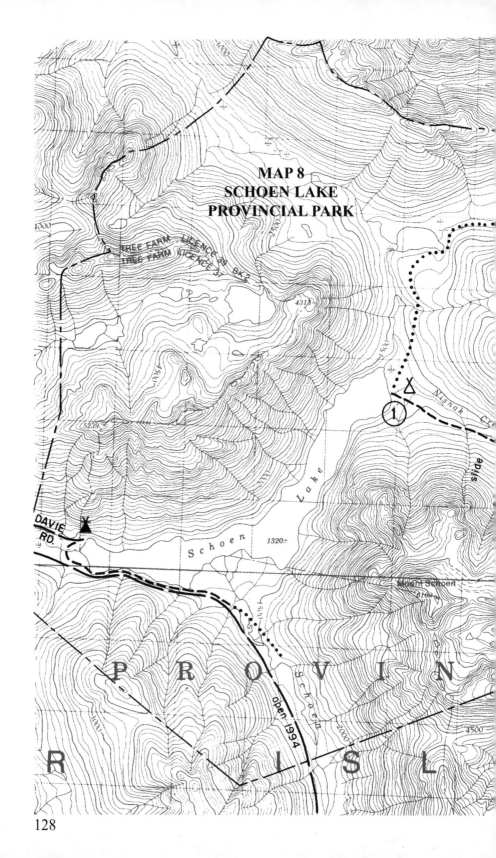

MAP 8
SCHOEN LAKE
PROVINCIAL PARK

128

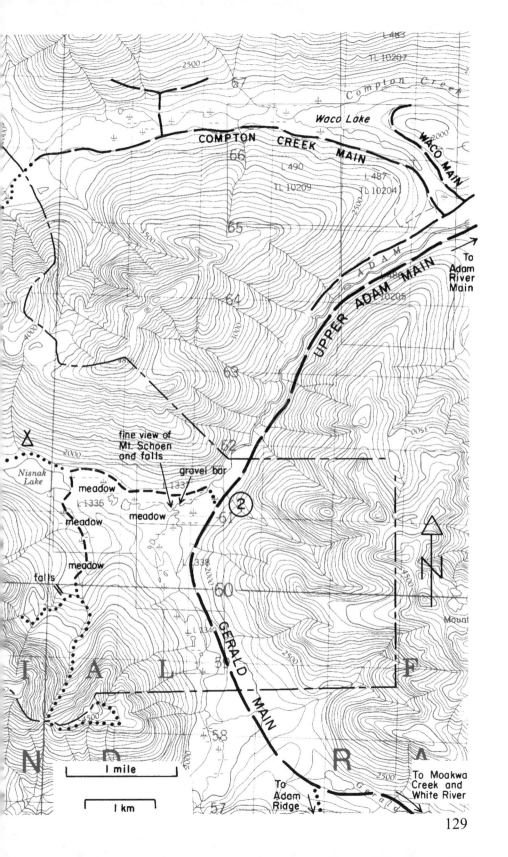

Compton Creek

TL 10207

L 483

2500

67

Waco Lake

WACO MAIN

2000

COMPTON CREEK MAIN

66

L 490

TL 10209

L 487

TL 10204

2500

N

2500

65

ADAM

UPPER ADAM MAIN

To Adam River Main

64

3000

TL 10205

3500

63

L 486

2000

fine view of Mt. Schoen and falls

62

gravel bar

Nisnak Lake

meadow

L 1336

133

meadow

②

61

meadow

L 338

N

falls

meadow

60

L 340

4500

I A L

L 339

GERALD MAIN

2500

F

2500

59

Mount

2500

1500

58

N D R A

1 mile

2000

57

To Adam Ridge

To Moakwa Creek and White River

Access to Schoen Lake Park from Upper Adam River (Map 8)

The access logging road is in Tree Farm Licence 39 administered by MacMillan Bloedel Ltd., Kelsey Bay Division. Drive north on the North Island Highway (19) from Kelsey Bay turn-off about 11 km to Keta Lake. Turn left onto Upper Adam River Main road and continue for about 22 km. There is active logging in Compton Creek, Adam and Gerald Lake areas. Upper Adam is an active haul road, so be aware of heavy logging traffic. In times of very high to extreme fire hazard, access is closed and at such times it would be wise to check beforehand with MacMillan Bloedel (see page 11).

A parking lot [2] (unsigned) has been constructed. A flagged route goes down to the river from here. Be prepared for wet footing and slippery log crossings. The closest established camping place is a single spot on the north side of Nisnak Lake (about 45 minutes backpack in). The Nisnak area is dominated by Mount Schoen with its snowfield and waterfalls. The falls drain into the southeastern corner of Nisnak Lake. Although not on a distinct trail, they can be reached by using the drainage route as a guide and by taking advantage of elk trails and traversing the meadows.

The curved ridge extending southeast from Mount Schoen can be climbed by following the steep gully that points south above the first falls. On the ridge there is easier snow walking and a fine view, and west from the col is a more challenging scramble toward the main peaks of Schoen. Further south, the long ridge extending east from Mount Adam can be climbed by heading south from Gerald Lake - about one hour to the ridge.

The Compton Creek route can be picked up off the end of Compton Creek Main and makes a good one-day circuit. It was an old trapline and is hard to locate on the ground, but there are still some old blazes. It can be used as an alternative to returning on the Nisnak Trail.

PORT HARDY AREA

Marble River Trail

Leave the North Island Highway 16 km north of Port McNeill, and take the paved highway towards Port Alice for 19 km. Turn right, immediately after crossing the bridge over Marble River, into a riverside parking area. Leave your vehicle here, and walk into the campground and follow the signs to the trail. The trail ends at the river, and it takes about 1 hour to walk to the end.

The Marble River trail offers a pleasant 3.7 km walk through mature hemlock/balsam forest, with access to the river. The trail stays on the bench, above a shallow canyon cut through the limestone rock by the action of the river. It is a very popular recreation spot, especially for steelhead fishing.

The campsite and trail were developed by Western Forest Products Ltd. In 1995, the provincial government set aside the river canyon area, estuary and adjacent lands at Varney Bay and Quatsino Narrows to be administered as a Provincial Park.

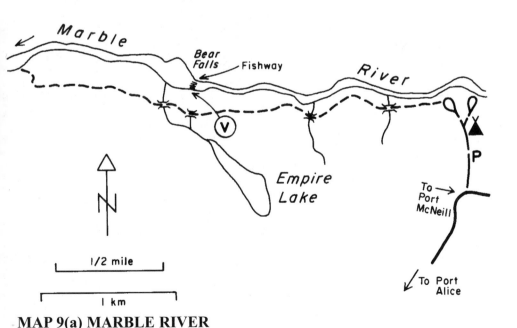

MAP 9(a) MARBLE RIVER

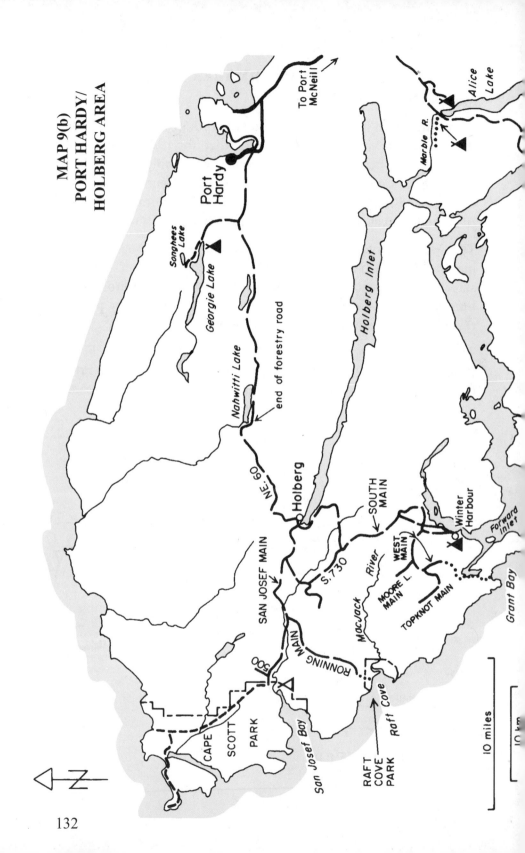

MAP 9(b)
PORT HARDY/
HOLBERG AREA

To Port McNeill

Alice Lake

Marble R.

Port Hardy

Songhees Lake

Georgie Lake

Holberg Inlet

Nahwitti Lake

end of forestry road

Holberg

NE. 60

SOUTH MAIN

Winter Harbour

Forward Inlet

WEST MAIN

MacJack River

S.730

MOORE L.
MAIN

Grant Bay

SAN JOSEF MAIN

TOPKNOT MAIN

RONNING MAIN

S500

Raft Cove

CAPE SCOTT PARK

San Josef Bay

RAFT COVE PARK

10 miles

10 km

N

Georgie Lake to Songhees Lake Trail (Map 9(b), page 132)

From Port Hardy drive on a forestry road about 8 km and turn right onto a fairly good gravel road. Follow this another 5 km to Georgie Lake. Active logging may be encountered. At Georgie Lake there is a sandy beach, and a campground administered by the BC Forest Service, with four campsites, wood supply and outhouses. An angler's trail, about 5 km long and in good shape, goes from here to Songhees Lake, where there is good fishing for cutthroat trout. The trail is suitable for all age groups.

HOLBERG AREA

To reach Cape Scott, Raft Cove or Grant Bay, exit the North Island Highway 3 km before Port Hardy (or 234 km from Campbell River) and then follow the roads as on Map 9(b), page 132.

Active logging is encountered the whole way. Access is open 24 hours a day, but obey all road signs. Logging trucks and crew vehicles have right of way. Travel with lights on. The Holberg logging division is administered by Western Forest Products Ltd. who may be contacted at Vancouver, Jeune Landing, Port McNeill and Holberg. They have an office in Holberg. You should get their most up-to-date recreation map (see page 11), which will show current active logging areas and their most recent roads, and read their information carefully. This map also details access to Cape Scott, Raft Cove, Grant Bay and eleven other major recreation sites including the much-recommended Marble River campsite with a trail along the river.

Travelling from Holberg to Winter Harbour, take logging road S730 then connect with South Main road. Check local conditions first.

Holberg has a gas station, a neighbourhood pub and a motel.

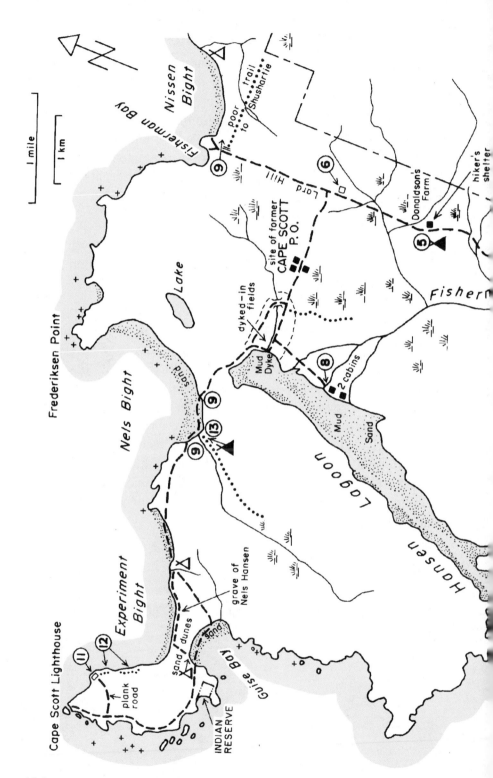

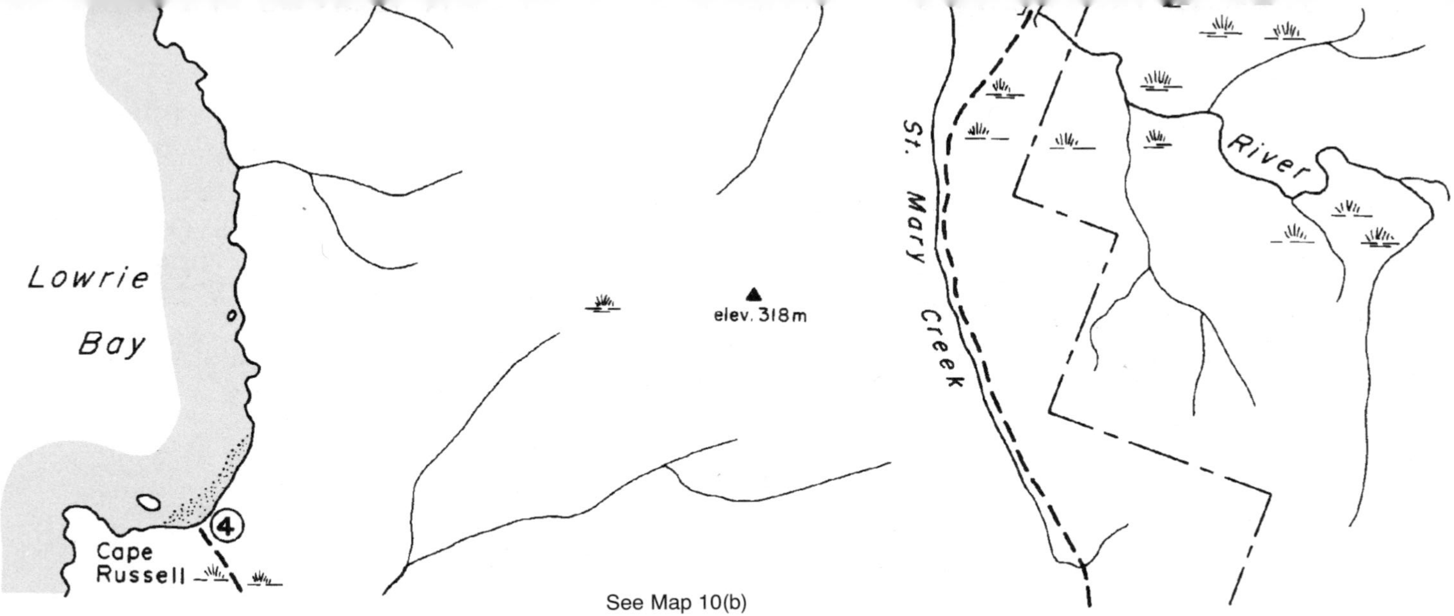

MAP 10(a) CAPE SCOTT PROVINCIAL PARK (north)

River

St. Mary Creek

elev. 318 m

See Map 10(b)

Lowrie Bay

Cape Russell

④

135

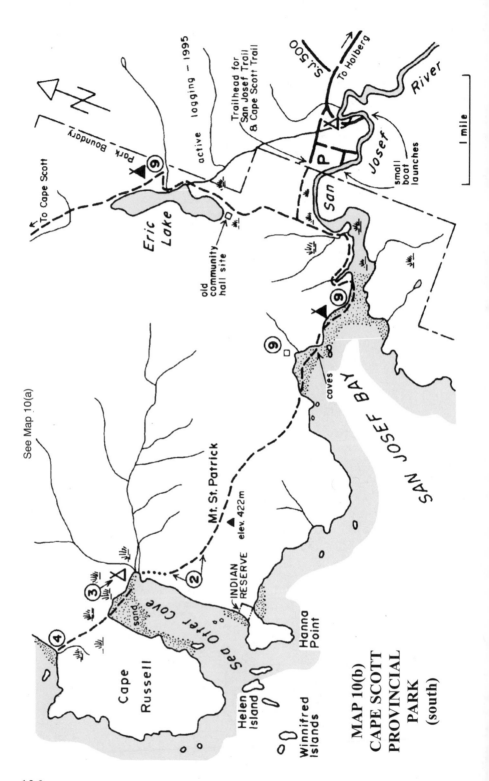

See Map 10(a)

active logging – 1995

Park Boundary

To Cape Scott

Eric Lake

old community hall site

Trailhead for San Josef Trail & Cape Scott Trail

S.J 500

To Holberg

San Josef

River

small boat launches

N

1 mile

Mt. St. Patrick
elev. 422m

INDIAN RESERVE

Hanna Point

caves

SAN JOSEF BAY

Cape Russell

Sea Otter Cove

sand

Helen Island

Winnifred Islands

**MAP 10(b)
CAPE SCOTT
PROVINCIAL
PARK
(south)**

CAPE SCOTT PARK

Distances and approximate hiking times in good weather from the parking lots.

	km	hours	
San Josef Bay	2.5	3/4	water, camping, outhouses
Eric Lake	3.0	1	fresh water, camping, outhouse, food cache
Fisherman River	9.3	3	outhouse
Nissen Bight	15.0	5	water at east end, camping, outhouse, food cache
Hansen Lagoon	14.7	5 1/2	
Nels Bight	16.8	6	good camping area, water from pipe, outhouses, Ranger Station, food caches
Experiment Bight	18.9	6 1/2	
Guise Bay	20.7	7	limited water, camping
Cape Scott	23.6	8	

Notations for circled numbers on maps:

2 Very steep section.

3 Camping spot. Grasses awash at high tide. Water.

4 Interesting forest, large burls and water.

5 One cabin. Water and pit toilet.

6 Christensen boy's grave in grove of trees by holly bushes.

8 Log crossing, submerged at high tide.

9 Pit toilets

11 Supply landing

12 Headland by-passes

13 Ranger cabin staffed in summer months.

CAPE SCOTT PROVINCIAL PARK

For access see Maps 10(a) and 10(b), pages 134-136.

From Port Hardy to the start of the trail is about 2 hours, about 65 km on rough roads. From Holberg drive 3 km to where the old road to CFB Holberg intersects, then follow San Josef Main to the end which is 500 m past the entrance of the campground provided by Western Forest Products. There is parking space at the start of the trails. When parking do not block other cars.

You would need about a week in the area to see everything. A good one-day hike may be made to San Josef Bay and as far as Eric Lake; persons going further in should be properly equipped with backpacking gear and food.

The whole park is a naturalist's paradise. Most of the trails are the old settlers' roads, some of which have been cleared out by the former CFS Holberg Ground Search Team as a 1971-72 Centennial Project. Regular upgrading is done by BC Parks Service. The Cape Scott Trail, now 23.6 km long, follows the settlers' trails and the old telephone line which ran from Holberg Inlet northwest to Cape Scott lighthouse, Fisherman Bay and Hansen Lagoon. The old telephone wire can still be seen in some locations.

The first part of the trail is in the Quatsino Rain Forest (annual rainfall between 380 cm and 510 cm) so here the trail is always muddy. The weather improves towards Cape Scott, but is always unpredictable and it can be downright chilly even in summer. Always be prepared for the unexpected.

The Cape Scott area is of immense historical interest, and the informative, historical interpretive signs at various locations in the park are well worth reading. Opened up by sturdy Danish settlers in the late 1890s, this was the scene of toil and disillusion. The settlers were gradually defeated in their efforts to homestead the land by the many hardships: the impossibility of getting produce to market, failure of the governments of the day to provide the promised road, stormy winters which made it difficult to land supply boats, cougars which devoured their domestic animals, and lack of medical help in emergencies.

But many of the settlers' clearings, roads and buildings are still visible for the hiker to marvel at. Most homes are now flat and all equipment has been removed except for the rusting remains of the heaviest implements. The one-time farmlands are deserted. There are countless side trails and old farm sites to discover - in fact, as many things as you have time to hunt for. Use caution when exploring: many of the settlers' wells still lie hidden.

San Josef Bay is beautiful with its wildlife marshes and acres of sandy beaches, and to camp at "San Jo" and explore this area makes an excellent trip. Most of the trail to San Josef is surfaced with gravel and well-graded. You can canoe the river from the Western Forest Products campsite. BC Parks has made a trail leading to the top of Mount St. Patrick (which affords a magnificent viewpoint). The top of this mountain is covered with crowberries. From here the trail leads to Sea Otter Cove, approximately 10 km; time-about $2^1/_2$ hours. Currently this trail has had little if any work done on it, except for faded markers that can be found on the trees. Fresh water is at the Cove, but you must bushwhack up the creek about 100 metres to go above the tides. From here it is about 2 km to Lowrie Bay.

Back on the main trail the first satisfactory camp spot from the start of the trail is on the gravel bar at the mouth of the creek running into Eric Lake. This is a scenic treasure, with warm swimming and fishing right at your feet.

Fisherman River has a good log bridge but you should be careful at some of the other creek crossings. Farther on you come to the obvious turn-off to Hansen Lagoon. The trail north continues through fairly open country of sphagnum bogs with cedar and hemlock small-growth vegetation, and then down "Lard Hill" through timber to Fisherman Bay and Nissen Bight. One is a gravelled bay with old wood shipwrecks; the other, 800 metres of clean white sand, with relatively small, evergreen growth to the foreshore. The Shushartie trail eastwards can be found with some difficulty about a quarter mile beyond the clay stretch of trail bed. It can be followed to the remains of a 340-m-long bridge over a lake (about 1.5 km).

Returning to Hansen Lagoon turn-off, hike to the former Cape Scott Post Office and farm (burned down in 1971), past the remains of the old community hall and down to the several hundred acres of flat meadowland at the Lagoon. These are of special interest to any visitor - dyked by the settlers with rock and fill to keep out the waters of the Lagoon. To get to the big surf beach, Nels Bight, take the trail to the right at the BC Parks sign at the meadow entrance.

Nels Bight has nearly 2 km of flat white sand with pounding surf. On the west side of the creek flowing out into Nels Bight a water pipe has been installed by the Parks staff in order to prevent pollution of the water supply. Do not rely on the creeks. Pit toilets have also been installed at two locations here as shown on our map. The ranger cabin is not for public use, but is a place from where the park rangers can work for extended periods of time.

Walk through to Guise Bay for another beautiful surf beach and from there go north through sand dunes to the jeep road leading for about 2 km through lush vegetation to the lighthouse. Read the notice at the lighthouse, walk up the driveway, and then down a boardwalk to the very tip of Vancouver Island. On returning to Guise Bay, walk across the sand dunes back to the northern shore, and return to Experiment Bight by trail along the beach past lovely little rocky coves, to make your hike at the Cape into a round trip. (Note - by going down the plank sideroad to the supply landing and out to the end of the longest guy wire, you can find a trail to the beach and return to the sand neck by beaches and headland by-pass trails).

At Guise Bay there are the remains of an RCAF camp from the Second World War years.

NOTES: BC Parks provides an excellent leaflet on Cape Scott Park which contains much useful information. You should read this before setting out on your trip. See page 11 for their addresses. Copies should also be available at some tourist information bureaus and from some sporting goods stores.

On logging roads give way to all heavy logging vehicles as they have right of way, and drive with your lights on so you can be seen through the dust clouds.

We stress that you must be completely self-sufficient from Holberg onwards: only in extreme emergency could help be forthcoming from logging camps. Help may be available from the Ranger Station at Nels Bight during the summer months. Similarly, though you may visit around the lighthouse at Cape Scott, do not expect any hospitality from the staff there. The lighthouse water supply is rainwater caught in cisterns, so they have no water to spare. Come well prepared and have a good week's supply of food.

Pack everything in plastic bags. Carry a rainproof tent, waterproof matches, firestarter, a small stove, and in summer bug repellent, change of clothing and socks. Plenty of warm dry clothing is more useful than a pair of heavy binoculars. Polypropylene, fleece or wool clothing will keep you warm even when wet and is essential for this location. A rain suit, taped at the ankles, will help to keep you clean - there is mud everywhere. Good boots and gaiters are essential for the mud (no running shoes), and even with that combination some people prefer to hike in shorts to stay cool.

Coastal hiking can be dangerous and is not recommended as many headlands are impassable. Knowledge of tides is essential. Coastal travel should not be attempted on a high or incoming tide. If you camp on a beach in this area, be careful to pitch your tent well above the high water mark. When backed by a wind, the incoming tides tend to be higher than is shown in the tide book.

During summer on the salt marsh flats at Hansen Lagoon there is a good growth of goose tongue (plantain) grass as well as the succulent "sea asparagus" which, when added to soups and stews, form a good dietary supplement to freeze-dried food.

Other Areas

There are mussels on the beaches which, though a bit tough, are edible - but no clams or oysters. Check with the Department of Fisheries about red tide (paralytic shellfish poisoning, or PSP) before consuming shellfish. Salmonberries, huckleberries and salal berries are plentiful in summer.

Leave cabins as you would like to find them - clean, and with a supply of dry wood for the next comers. Take your litter out with you and leave nothing to attract bears and small animals. Bury all excrement (while we're on the subject). Respect private property and Indian Reserves within the Park.

No hunting within the Park.

When driving up to Port Hardy you may find it useful to camp overnight at one of the many BC Forest Service Recreation Sites. The BCFS provides free maps of excellent quality. For this area you will need the Port McNeill Forest District map. In Victoria these are available at the Ministry of Forest Recreation Branch office on Government Street at Johnson.

Flying in is only allowed with a permit from BC Parks.

If you are planning to use the beaches, take a tide table (Pacific Coast Tide and Current Tables, Vol. 6) available from Crown Publications, in Victoria (386-4636) or from most sporting goods stores.

Cougars and black bears frequent the area. Hang your food at night and when you are away from camp. Keep dogs on a leash.

RAFT COVE PROVINCIAL PARK

Isolated on the northwest coast of Vancouver Island, south of Cape Scott Park, Raft Cove Park is distinguished by its 1.3 km length of open beach. The cove offers little protection from the winds, and the Pacific surf pounds its shores endlessly. The Macjack River meanders into the ocean at the south end of the beach. A narrow but forested peninsula separates the Pacific on the west from the Macjack on the east .

Access: See Map 9(b) (page 132). Along the road, read advisory signs carefully. Parking is available at the trailhead. Follow signs along the Holberg road, and obey all signs and rules of the road in this busy, industrial traffic area. Tourists maps are available from Western Forest Products (see page 11).

New Trail (Map 11, page 144)

A recently-constructed logging road has made Raft Cove accessible by a new 1.2 km route which takes 45 minutes to hike. The route begins at the end of "Ronning 700" and is marked with orange ribbons.

Canoe/kayak access can be gained by entering the Macjack River from the Winter Harbour road systems.

The cabin on the south side of the Macjack is Willie Hecht's old trapping cabin. It is mouse-ridden, but still useable with a small stove, four bunk beds and a table. According to L.R. Peterson's "Cape Scott Story" (pp. 81, 93 and 108), Hecht and the Boytle family were the pioneers of the Macjack settlement in 1913, but by the early twenties only Hecht was left. As early as 1909 a trail had been established from Raft Cove up Ronning Creek to the San Josef-Holberg trail.

Summer tenters will most enjoy camping on Raft Cove beach. Here they will have the crashing surf, and beyond they can watch the freighters pass and see the distant fish boats silhouetted against the horizon. The best water is available from the stream emptying into the south side of the Macjack near the cabin.

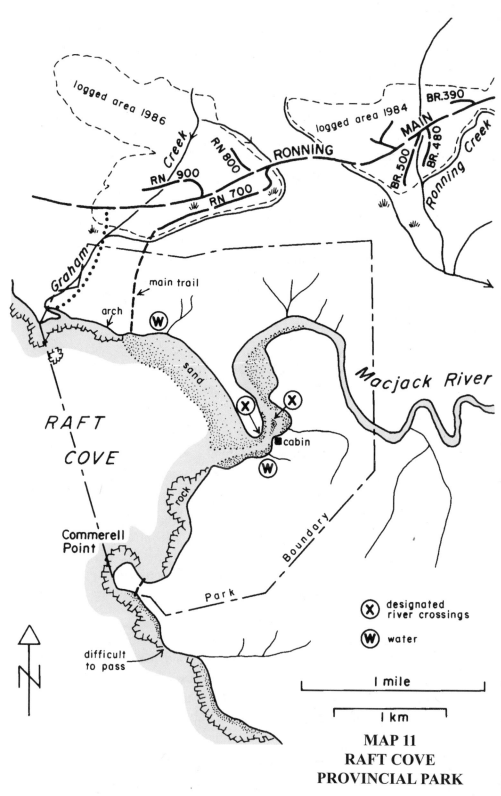

logged area 1986

RN Creek

RN 900

RN 800

RN 700

RONNING

logged area 1984

MAIN

BR.390

BR.500

BR.480

Ronning Creek

Graham

main trail

arch

W

sand

Macjack River

X

X

cabin

RAFT

COVE

W

rock

Commerell
Point

Boundary

Park

difficult
to pass

N

X designated
river crossings

W water

1 mile

1 km

**MAP 11
RAFT COVE
PROVINCIAL PARK**

During low tides, shore walks can be made both north and south of Raft Cove. To the south, where small islands of jagged tidal rock stand in sharp contrast to the sands of Raft Cove, an easy 2.2 km walk is possible. The easy walking ends south of Commerell Point where there is a choice of either slippery rocks or a steep salal-overgrown slope. Commerell Point itself can be crossed at its neck by a trail marked with blue ribbons.

Dan Hicks

GRANT BAY

Grant Bay is an isolated little bay on the north side of the entrance to Quatsino Sound. Bounded by a shore of shoals and rock, its main attraction is 800 m of sandy beach. Hiking time one way - 2½ hours by land route or one hour by sea route.

Access: See Map 9(b), page 132 and read Holberg Area section carefully. The road to Holberg is good. South Main to Winter Harbour is a main haul road to Holberg, so expect to meet logging traffic.

Someone with a small boat can launch it at Winter Harbour, go down Forward Inlet, then up Browning Inlet, a distance by sea of 9 km. (Editor's note: Philip Stooke warns, in his book "Landmarks and Legends of the North Island" that at high tide at Quatleyo Point (the tip of the Indian Reserve) there is an extensive hidden rock ledge which must be avoided. He recommends landing near the north end of the bay.) However, if planning to return at high tide, the boater will be able to get within 220 m of the start of the Browning Inlet/Grant Bay section of the trail. The walk to the bay from the Inlet is only half an hour; sturdy boots are an advantage.

Winter Harbour itself is a quaint little fishing village complete with a boardwalk, well-kept old houses, three wharves, a store, restaurant, and a hotel. Just north of the village is a seaside campsite guarded by a brightly-coloured, eagle-topped totem pole.

Turn right at West Main/South Main junction, just north of Winter Harbour. Follow posted signs to the trailhead.

Keep your lights on and anticipate meeting a truck on every turn. After travelling about 6 km on West Main, at junction with Topknot Main, take left fork continuing on West Main. Go 2 km south along this and you will see West 71 branch road on the left.

Map 12, page 147. About 70 m beyond the W.71 turnoff, on the right hand side of the road, is Branch W.73, the beginning of the trail. In 1994, the alders, in the section of the trail which follows the old roads, were brushed out. WFP reports that a new trailhead will be in place by the end of 1996. Hiking time from here to Browning Inlet is approximately 1 hour and 40 minutes.

Stay on the road through the clearcut. Keep right and avoid the left spur which angles up the hill. After about 25 minutes, you can locate the trail south through 100 m of clearcut slash to the timber. This trail is a popular route for black bears and the inlet itself is a preferred hangout for them. But they are unlikely to be a problem as they are genuinely wild and associate man with danger and not with food.

In the timber the trail is established and obvious; faded red and blue ribbons give an additional assurance. The forest type is mature hemlock/balsam with some cedar. Within 20 minutes the hiker reaches a blowdown zone, a maze of uprooted trees blown over by the wind. Different trails have been ribboned through the fallen trees. Take care to identify the trail again on the south side of the blowdown; it is as obvious as it was on the north side. From here to Kwatleo Creek is only 10 minutes and Browning Inlet a further 35 minutes. The hiker descends into the creek gully and crosses the creek on a large log against which smaller logs have been jammed. On the south side of this natural bridge the trail parallels the creek.

Future development by WFP will result in a road connection from West Main (just north of W 70) to this point, and a parking lot.

Follow the faded ribbons and avoid two trails to the left. Encroaching salmonberry crowds the trail in a section at the creek's mouth into the inlet. A different timber type emerges at Kwatleo Creek - a larger diameter spruce/cedar forest. The spruce trees are especially majestic and impressive.

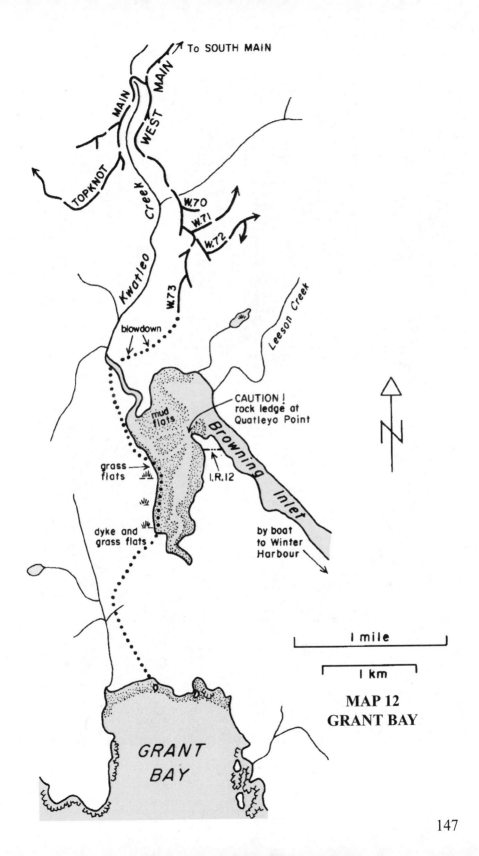

To SOUTH MAIN

MAIN

WEST MAIN

TOPKNOT

Kwatleo Creek

W.70

W.71

W.72

W.73

blowdown

Leeson Creek

mud flats

CAUTION!
rock ledge at
Quatleyo Point

Browning Inlet

grass flats

I.R.12

dyke and
grass flats

by boat
to Winter
Harbour

N

1 mile

1 km

**MAP 12
GRANT BAY**

GRANT
BAY

147

Grant Bay

The Kwatleo Creek trail drops the hiker onto the grassy fringe of the great tidal mud flat that is the head of Browning Inlet. The trail to Grant Bay begins in the southwest corner of the inlet head and is marked by a blue plastic jug in an old fruit tree. This old fruit tree and its neighbours, together with a dyke, are the epitaphs to a failed attempt at cultivation. The 50 cm high dyke extends into the grassy fringe north and east from the forest for 80 m and 90 m respectively. While moving on one should look back at this location a few times so as to identify it easily when returning. Walk on the relatively firm tidal mud rather than the grassy fringe which has many small but hazardous natural ditches.

Grant Bay is only 30 minutes from the inlet on this final trail which is common to both the land and the sea route. Salal lines the muddy first half of the trail, which winds through a spike-topped cedar/hemlock forest with scattered large balsams. The second half of the trail is better. The trail is drier and more open; sword fern, deer fern and salmonberry are common plants. The forest is a spruce/hemlock type, with very large spruce trees.

The shining smooth sands of Grant Bay contrast sharply with the terrain previously travelled. Water is available from the stream at the west end of the beach - poor-tasting cedar water, but drinkable (and should be boiled). The stream mouth is jammed with sea logs. The derelict shack east of the creek lets in as much rain as it keeps out. No camper should contemplate staying in it. Tents should be placed high on the beach, safe from summer high tides.

Facing south, Grant Bay is less exposed to the open Pacific, and its surf is moderate compared to the exposed west coast beaches. In close visual proximity from east to west, one can see Cape Parkins, Kwakiutl Point and Cape Cook at the end of Brooks Peninsula. Shore travel from Grant Bay beach is difficult; the adjacent shores are all rock. The only exception is a small isolated beach on the east side of the rocky point on Grant Bay beach's east end. Just relax and enjoy the sand and sun while watching the freighters and fish boats pass by.

Dan Hicks

About the Friends of Strathcona Park

F.O.S.P. is a non-profit society with an interest in Strathcona Provincial Park. Stewardship of the park is the key objective of The Friends, and they actively support the management directives described by Strathcona Park's Master Plan. Present activities centre on supporting proposed additions to Strathcona Park, and include discussions with forest industry companies which own land on the park's boundaries. The Friends of Strathcona Park also sponsors trail building projects, and has formally "adopted" the Bedwell River Trail.

About the Strathcona Wilderness Institute

The Strathcona Wilderness Institute (SWI) is a non-profit society which, through public education, promotes an appreciation and awareness of the natural world - particularly in and around Strathcona Park on Vancouver Island. SWI operates under a cooperative agreement with BC Parks.

The Institute's year-round public education program includes lectures, exhibitions, special events, research projects and publications, as well as educational courses such as Wilderness Self-Reliance, Medicinal Plants, Geology in Strathcona Park, Fall Birding and Coast to Coast Treks.

Interest in creating a Wilderness Institute resulted from a 1992 conference at Strathcona Park Lodge, organized by the F.O.S.P. and attended by representatives from forestry, tourism, education and parks sectors. The conference focused on society's relationship to wilderness.

What emerged was a major concern to protect existing wilderness areas, and how this could be done. Based on agreement at this conference that society in general needs to be more knowledgeable about, and more in contact with, the natural world, the Strathcona Wilderness Institute was formed in 1994.

For more information, and a brochure, write to S.W.I., Box 3404, Courtenay, BC, V9N 5N5 or phone/fax (604) 337-8220.

INDEX

Note: **Bold print** indicates a map reference.

List of Photographs